D0841087

LEARN
TALMUD

LEARN TALMUD

How to Use
The Talmud
The Steinsaltz Edition

Judith Z. Abrams

JASON ARONSON INC.
Northvale, New Jersey
London

The author gratefully acknowledges permission to reprint the following:

Excerpt from SIFRE ON DEUTERONOMY, translated by Reuven Hammer. Copyright © 1986 Yale University. Reprinted by permission of Yale University Press, publisher.

Select verses from THE BABYLONIAN TALMUD, edited by I. Epstein. Copyright © 1936. Reprinted by permission of The Soncino Press, Ltd., publisher.

This book was set in 11 pt. Palatino by Alpha Graphics of Pittsfield, New Hampshire, and printed by Haddon Craftsmen in Scranton, Pennsylvania.

Copyright © 1995 Judith Z. Abrams

10 9 8 7 6 5 4 3 2 1

All rights reserved. Printed in the United States of America. No part of this book may be used or reproduced in any manner whatsoever without written permission from Jason Aronson Inc. except in the case of brief quotations in reviews for inclusion in a magazine, newspaper, or broadcast.

Library of Congress Cataloging-in-Publication Data

Abrams, Judith Z.
    Learn Talmud : How to Use *The Talmud—The Steinsaltz Edition* / by Judith Z. Abrams.
      p.   cm.
    "Selected passages, which are among the most accessible in the two
tractates presently translated by Rabbi Steinsaltz, are presented
with aids for study"—Introd.
    Includes bibliographical references and index.
    ISBN 1-56821-463-4
    1. Talmud. English—Versions—Steinsaltz. 2. Talmud—
Introductions. 3. Talmud—Study and teaching. 4. Talmud—
Outlines, syllabi, etc. I. Steinsaltz, Adin. II. Talmud.
English. Selections. III. Title.
BM499.5.E4   1989a
296.1'250521—dc20
                             94-45558
                             CIP

Manufactured in the United States of America. Jason Aronson Inc. offers books and cassettes. For information and catalog write to Jason Aronson Inc., 230 Livingston Street, Northvale, New Jersey 07647.

For My Talmud Teachers:

Professor Jakob J. Petuchowski, *zakhor l'tov*

Rabbi Joseph Radinsky

Professor Avraham Amir

Professor David Kraemer

Contents

1 Introduction

2 Course Outlines

3 The Passages

4 Material from Volumes Still to Come

Acknowledgments

As always, I am grateful to God for the opportunity to write this book. I am especially grateful to Arthur Kurzweil of Jason Aronson Inc., who asked me to write it. I must thank Arthur, too, for his helpful comments on the manuscript, as well as Rabbi Joseph Radinsky for the same. Marion Cino helped in the preparation with her characteristic warmth and charm, as did Muriel Jorgensen in the editorial department. I am beholden to the students to whom I taught this material, both at Congregation Beth El in Missouri City, Texas: Naomi and Eyal Enav, Jeannie Krim, Ronit Linzer, Lisa Mengler, and Janice Poscovsky; and at the Jewish Federation in Houston: Jeanne Bijou, Linda Burger, Sharon Clark, Vivian Coggan, Dana Gavin, Jody Hirsch, Suzanne Jacobsen, Frances T. Kleese, Amelia R. Kleiman, Carla Muller, Deborah Ostroff, Sue Riklin, Marsha Schooler, Sophie Scharfsman, Jeff Sokoloff, Michael Steinberg, Freda Tiras, and Jude Wolf. I learn the most from my students! I also want to thank Tanya Perelshtyn and Elizabeth Vainrub for their help.

Finally, I want to thank my husband, Steven, and my children, Michael, Ruth, and Hannah, for making it possible for me to write this book.

1

Introduction

HAVING A HARD TIME GETTING STARTED?

You bought these beautiful books: *The Talmud: The Steinsaltz Edition*. Hurray for you! That's a big investment in an important Jewish resource. You thought, "Wow! I'm finally going to discover why the Talmud has been the treasure of the Jewish people for 1,500 years!" You couldn't wait to jump in. You opened up a volume and started reading. But figuring out the page, which didn't look like any page you'd ever studied, was difficult. And then there was the material. Some of it was simply bizarre. Parts of it were interesting but it was hard to get a feel for the stuff. You became discouraged and looked at it less and less until the set of books began to just sit there on the shelf looking pretty and feeling inaccessible. Your previous feelings of curiosity and hope were replaced by disappointment and frustration and feelings of low self-esteem . . . and maybe a little anger.

Why is the Talmud so hard!?! It's hard because the sages who put it together wanted you to study it only with a teacher. So they made it almost impossible to study by yourself. To study Talmud is not just to read a book. It is to become a member of a select society of scholars and spiritual seekers. Jumping into Talmud study the first time is a bit of an initiation rite and might even feel like hazing. Whether you ultimately join the ranks of those who are in love with the Talmud or become one of the larger group who never understand its beauty is up to you as an individual.

That decision depends on the gifts God has given you, where you are in your spiritual journey in life, and how much you are motivated to find the beauty that is in the Talmud.

This book is designed to help you over the initial hurdles of Talmud study. In it, selected passages, which are among the most accessible in the two tractates presently translated by Rabbi Steinsaltz, are presented with aids for study. You might be able to enter the world of the Talmud with just the Steinsaltz translation and the aid of this book alone. However, I urge you to study with a teacher. If you cannot study with a teacher, then study with a friend who knows as much as you do. If you cannot study with an equal, then study with someone you can teach.

TALMUD STUDY AND RELATIONSHIPS

Talmud study is not just about enriching your mind. It's about building relationships through the beauty of our tradition. It's about finding something really nice in everyone you study with. There is a very famous saying about how to study Talmud: "Provide yourself with a teacher; get yourself a companion; and judge every person charitably" (*Avot* 1:6). You could reinterpret this to mean, "When you have a teacher, you also have a friend and you find it easier to see the best in others." This is what Talmud study is really about. The first person you learn to love when you study Talmud, believe it or not, is yourself. However, you also usually end up thinking well of the people you study with. Frankly, I would urge Jewish singles groups to study Talmud as one of their main activities. It would serve two purposes: Jews would come out of each session more knowledgeable about Judaism, and I suspect that a few matches would be made along the way.

"I AM LOVABLE, I AM CAPABLE"

The first thing to learn, before you even crack open a volume of the Talmud, is patience and love for yourself. You have to believe that you are worth spending lots of time on because Talmud study takes lots of time and benefits you directly. You have to believe that any amount of Talmud you study is a terrific achievement: if you started with zero Talmud knowledge, then every word you learn is a 100 percent improvement! In other words, you have to have an appropriate amount of self-esteem. How can you achieve that state of mind? The sages show us the way:

> "Love your neighbor as yourself" (Leviticus 19:18). Rabbi Akiva said: This is the greatest principle in the Torah. Ben Azzai quoted the verse: "This is the book of the generations of Adam. In that day God created human beings; in the likeness of God did God make him" (Genesis 5:1). He said: This is a principle greater than that. (*Sifra* on Leviticus 19:18)

Why is the most important verse in the Torah that we are created in God's image rather than loving our neighbor as ourselves? Because if you don't love yourself, then you won't treat yourself the way you should and you won't treat your neighbor the way you should, either. However, if you remember that every creature is created in God's image, even you, then you'll treat everyone the way they should be treated.

When you begin studying Talmud you run through a range of emotions, one of which is impatience with yourself, stemming from low self-esteem. You think, "I ought to be able to understand this more quickly than I am. Gosh, I must be dumb." No, you are not dumb. This is harder than you think and it's going to take longer than you think. When you start feeling this way, say to yourself or as a class together, "I am lovable. I am capable. I am lovable. I am capable." It will hopefully make you laugh so that you can put things in perspective and get back to the task at hand, refreshed.[1]

THE TRAP OF THE INTELLECT

If you'll notice, I said that everyone ought to have an appropriate level of self-esteem when approaching the Talmud. Most of us have the problem of self-esteem that's too low. However, a few

---

1. See Sidney Simon's book, *I am Loveable and Capable* (Niles, IL: Argus Communications, 1974).

of us have self-esteem that's too high, especially for intellectual tasks. If you are smart and are used to conquering problems with your intellect, watch out! You are about to fall into the biggest trap of Talmud study. You are about to think, "I can conquer this material with my brain!" No! *You cannot outsmart the Talmud.* If you think you're outsmarting it, you're just fooling yourself. What you are experiencing is your own ego getting in the way of really studying the Talmud. If you are more interested in your own insights than in what the Talmud has to say, you're not getting all you could out of the Talmud. It's not that the Talmud shouldn't be relevant to your life. But your life and the Talmud should form a duet in your soul. If you are the melody and the Talmud is a faint harmony, then you aren't really studying Talmud. Talmud is just giving you an excuse to listen to yourself. And, if you'll forgive me, the people in the Talmud deserve a good bit of your attention. Listen to them as well as to yourself.

Talmud study involves a balancing act. If your self-esteem is too low, you'll give up. If your self-esteem is too high, you won't ever really engage in meaningful Talmud study. The trick is to come to it with a healthy regard for yourself and a healthy respect for the people who will teach you from the Talmud's pages. Keep juggling your humility and your hubris and eventually you'll achieve the correct balance. By the way, if this is all you ever get from Talmud study, you'll still have achieved a great deal!

FEELING ALL RIGHT
ABOUT FEELING UNCOMFORTABLE

Sometimes we have the misconception that something that is "religious" and "inspirational," such as the Talmud, is something that we're going to feel uniformly positively about. This is simply not the case with Talmud. You are going to read things in the passages presented here that you wish you hadn't read. Sometimes the sages seem to be permitting behavior that just doesn't seem right. You'll think to yourself, "I'm embarrassed by what I just read." Or you'll think, "I don't agree with this at all. How could they say that?"

When you read something like this it is often helpful to examine the nature of the statement you are reading. Is it theory or is it case law? Is it an academic discussion designed to teach students or is this going to be enforced in the general population? Is this a story (Midrash or Aggadah) or is it law (Halakhah)? You can also occasionally ease your feelings of discomfort by looking at the Halakhah entries at the bottom of the page to see what became of the statement in Jewish law.

In classes on this material, I have used the "thirty-second–mad" rule. When the class encounters something sexist or troubling, I allow everyone to be mad for a maximum of thirty seconds. Then we get on with the business at hand and start trying to understand the text. There's no use getting stuck in the "mad mode." It just isn't productive. On the other hand, there's no reason to utterly suppress it. Just limit it.

When you feel uncomfortable or upset or you want to argue with the sages . . . you've hit the jackpot! That's how you *should* feel when you're studying Talmud: totally engaged because it matters. The goal is not to feel good all the time while studying Talmud (you will feel good most of the time, anyway). The goal is to feel alive, Jewishly alive.

I'd also like to point out one other thing. Much of what you are going to read in the Talmud is wise advice for living. In fact, it's so wise that many modern self-help books simply paraphrase Talmudic principles. So why would you want to study Talmud, which sometimes upsets you, rather than self-help books, which rarely do? For the same reason that you'd want to eat brown rice instead of white rice. White rice is bland and inoffensive but it doesn't have a great deal of nutritional value. Brown rice has more flavor and more nutrients but you have to chew it a little longer and it might be tougher. Just so, you might have to "chew on" the Talmud, that is, give it more thought and effort, than self-help literature, but in the end it's less processed and a lot better for you.

FEELING ALL RIGHT ABOUT LAUGHING

Another thing that may surprise you about the Talmud is that parts of it can be quite funny and fun. We have this image of Talmud as serious and intense—and it is. But it also contains humorous stories and playful passages. Sometimes I feel that newcomers to Talmud are like people unfamiliar with opera. People unfamiliar with opera assume it's going to be occasionally inspirational, probably boring, and rarely entertaining. They don't permit themselves to laugh even when something funny is going on. Let yourself laugh when something is funny. Let yourself feel entertained when the sages are being playful. Fun and playfulness are also part of being Jewishly alive.

READING RIGHT TO LEFT AND AROUND

A page of Talmud can be an intimidating thing, especially the way this edition of it is laid out. Go ahead and take out Volume III and turn to page 243. This looks almost nothing like an English book, which is read from left to right, top to bottom. You read a page of Talmud *around*. You also read it more than once if you're really going to learn. The main thing you're going to study, if you don't know Hebrew, is the Translation and Commentary, which is on the left-hand part of the page. Each sentence in the actual text of the Talmud, in the middle of the page in Hebrew letters, is numbered. The numbers in the Translation and Commentary and Literal Translation are coordinated with this central text. The bold-face type in the Translation and Commentary is the translation of the text. The rest, in plain type, is the commentary. It is occasionally fruitful to read the Literal Translation and compare it with the Translation and Commentary to see how much "filling in" needs to be done to bridge the gap between the sages' days and our own.

The Notes at the bottom of the page are Rabbi Steinsaltz's digested form of a massive number of medieval (and later) commentaries to the text. A list of these commentaries is in the back of each volume. If I were you, I'd ignore who said what for now and just concentrate on what they said. You can always go back later and figure out who the *Ra'avad* and the *Rosh* were. Every time you don't understand something in the Translation, check the bottom or side of the page to see if Rabbi Steinsaltz has written a note on it. You'll know there's a note because the bold-face type at the beginning of each Note entry tells you what line it refers to.

Under the Notes is a section entitled Halakhah. Halakhah is Jewish law and here Rabbi Steinsaltz summarizes the "bottom line," as it were, from the topics on the page. If you are interested in Jewish law, read these sections. If you are not interested in Jewish law, you may want to skip these entries until it becomes a subject that interests you.

On the outer margins are various sorts of notes that Rabbi Steinsaltz provides to help us study. Some of these will be more helpful to the beginning student and some more for the advanced student. If you are a beginner, stick to the entries marked Background, Sages, and Realia. If you are advanced, that is, you are starting to try to read the text in the original Hebrew and Aramaic, then go ahead and start reading the entries entitled Terminology and Language.

There is another Hebrew text on this page entitled Rashi. This is the classic medieval commentary to the Talmud, presented in the traditional script, which, you'll notice, is different from a standard Hebrew script. If you want to learn to read this script, the *Reference Guide* shows you the modern Hebrew equivalents (see pp. 301–302). Unless you are well advanced, you probably won't even be attempting to read this commentary. In many cases, Rabbi Steinsaltz's commentary includes Rashi's insights, so don't feel that you're losing too much by not reading Rashi separately.

Let's look at another page in this volume, page 250. We see, once more, the text in Hebrew and Aramaic in the center, the Literal Translation toward the spine of the book, and the Translation and Commentary toward the edges. Here, we have an entry entitled Realia on the side. As you'd expect, such entries describe, and sometimes illustrate, as here, the real world the sages were living in. Because the Gemara is describing concrete, specific items and procedures, there is a bit more trouble defining words, as reflected in the relatively large number of Language and Language (Rashi) entries. If you look over in the Rashi text, you'll see that the words listed in the Language (Rashi) entries are marked with successively greater numbers of stars. The Sages entry on this page gives you information on two of the sages cited in this discussion. At the very end of the chapter, on page 251, you'll see the words (in Hebrew) *hadran alakh hazahav*, "we will return unto you gold." This is an example of the formula that is said at the end of every chapter of Talmud. Each chapter's name is the first one or two words of the first Mishnah therein. At the end of a chapter, we vow to return again to this material. It's a way of reminding yourself that you're never finished studying Talmud.

How you read a page depends on what kind of learner you are. You might want to start with the Literal Translation, then the Translation and Commentary, and then the Notes. Or you might want to start with the Translation and Commentary and then go on to the Notes. You might want to read the Background Notes only. You may never get to the center of the page. Find your own entranceway to the page and spread out from there. One thing you may want to do is have a pencil in hand and/or some colored highlighting markers, if that's your style. Writing your own commentary in the margin is an honorable Jewish tradition. The book should really be distinctively yours by the time you're done. Your insights should be there for the next generation to build on.

THE *REFERENCE GUIDE*

Rabbi Steinsaltz has compiled an enormous amount of material in the *Reference Guide*. However, looking through the book might be daunting for a beginner because many of its sections are organized according to the Hebrew alphabet. Therefore, I'd like to steer you toward those parts of the *Guide* that will be of more relevance to you as you start studying Talmud.

Rabbi Steinsaltz's Introduction to the Talmud begins on page 1. It is a wonderful introduction, but you should know that other scholars have other thoughts on the Talmud's nature. This is as it should be. Rarely does an opinion stand unopposed or unrefined in the Talmud, and that same dynamic applies to modern scholarship and thought about the Talmud. Read this as a good introduction and later you can read other works that express different opinions. See the For Further Reading section for some options.

The introduction to the history of the period (pp. 11–24) would be good for you to read on your own before you start studying the text with a class. It is a very fine overview of the history, politics, and sociology of the era. Naturally, there are myriad volumes written on this topic and, again, you should hope to read some of those works in time. See the For Further Reading section for suggestions in this area.

The listing of Jewish communities, which begins on page 25, will be useful to you as you encounter these place names in the text. Often, the material here will be cited on the edges of the page of Talmud you're studying. You probably don't need to go over this section before you begin. Likewise, the chapter on the generations of the Tannaim and the Amoraim is one you can refer to as you become more advanced and are interested in the relationships of the sages to each other and their era. The list of the tractates of the Mishnah and the Talmud (pp. 37–47) might be nice for you to skim, just to get a feeling for the breadth of the tradition's area of inquiry. On pages 49–59, Rabbi Steinsaltz shows you how to read a traditional page of the Talmud. (This is somewhat ironic since his Hebrew translation of the Talmud, I predict, will in a very short time overtake this traditional form in popularity, except in scholarly communities. However, it's always nice to go back to the basics.) If you are about to embark on studying the Hebrew/Aramaic text of the Talmud, you might want to look at this information just to become oriented. This outline of the Talmudic page is especially nice because it shows how many generations of brilliant thinkers have found their way into the Talmud's pages. It's actually pretty humbling. You open a page of Talmud and you're in the presence of these giants. Don't worry—they're friendly giants who are glad to see you!

Pages 61–77, which outline Aramaic grammar and vocabulary, should interest you if you are starting to work with the Hebrew/Aramaic text. Aramaic and Hebrew are related. You might think of it as similar to the way American, British, and Australian English are related to each other. They are definitely in the same family but each has distinctive traits. If you aren't working with the Hebrew/Aramaic text of the Talmud, skip this section.

The Guidelines for Talmudic Study (pp. 79–87) is an important section and should be read before you begin your study. Rabbi Steinsaltz's words here are especially encouraging for a beginner. He helps introduce you to the proper mindset for Talmudic study. In essence, what he's saying is that through this English translation, he's going to introduce you to some of his dearest and most respected friends (the sages). It's as if he's with you at the door that will lead to the best party you've ever attended. Your hand is on the doorknob and you can't wait to enter. But Rabbi Steinsaltz puts his hand out to yours and just gives you a guide to the etiquette you'll need to follow to enjoy the party to the fullest. Once you read this, in you go!

Next, in the *Reference Guide*, come Mishnaic Methodology, Talmudic Terminology, and Talmudic Hermeneutics (pp. 89–154). Again, I would skip these sections until you are beginning to read the middle of the page. This material is rather technical and is going to feel pretty daunting if you're just starting out. Instead, I'd suggest taking a little time and skimming through the Halakhic Concepts and Terms, which begins on page 155. Just wander through this very long section and pick up on those items that seem interesting now; leave the others for later. There is an amazing amount of information here and it can give you a feel for the sages' world. You might want to start with one entry that interests you and follow the "prompts" to other entries. (Any word cited in the entry that has an asterisk by it has its own, separate, entry.)

The chapter on Talmudic Weights and Measures (pp. 279–293) will be crucial to the study of some Talmudic passages presented in this book. You needn't memorize these systems, but it's nice to have an idea of what's going on in this regard. The chapter entitled "Rules Governing Halakhic Decision-Making" is interesting, particularly if you are relating to the Talmud as a source of authoritative Jewish law. If you are interested in Halakhah, you'll enjoy this chapter. Even if you *aren't* interested in Halakhah, you'll probably enjoy this chapter! The rest of the *Reference Guide* is self-explanatory: *Rashi* script, abbreviations, and an index that you'll use as needed.

Some people enjoy studying the *Reference Guide* all by itself. Others study the translation and consult the *Reference Guide*. Still others just concentrate on the translation alone and never consult the *Reference Guide*. Just find out what is most helpful for you and follow that path.

A NEW DEFINITION OF PROGRESS

We expect so much in our lives to happen quickly. We expect to be able to read a book in a few days. We are seldom asked to struggle intellectually or spiritually. Things are made accessible for us.

Talmud study isn't like that. Talmud takes time. Talmud can put you off at first glance. Talmud study is rewarding, in part, because you have to work so hard at it. Before you begin studying Talmud you need to adjust your speed setting, so to speak. In Talmud study, an hour spent on just one page can mean you're going at a pretty good rate. You may have to go back to the same page several times in order to fully comprehend it. Six sessions on one passage is not a large amount of time to spend at all.

That said, it's important, as a beginner, to allow yourself to skip those passages or parts of passages that are too difficult to understand. The sages themselves understood that you can only truly study what speaks to you at this moment in your life:

> "But whose desire is in the law of the Lord" (Psalm 1:2). Said Rabbi: A man can learn only that part of the Torah that is his heart's desire, for it is said, "But whose *desire* is in the law of the Lord." (*Avodah Zarah* 19a)

Study what you want and leave the rest. If you keep at it long enough, you'll be able to come back to those parts you've skipped and find them meaningful. If you keep going at them now, they'll just make you feel bad because you don't understand them.

Take the journey in stages. If you're just starting, it will be like flying over a mountain range in an airliner. You'll see the dramatic highlights with little detail. Your next pass through the material will be like going through that same mountain range in a helicopter. You'll be closer to the action and see more of the character of the place. The next time through will be like driving on the mountain. Now you'll be in direct contact with the terrain. The next time you go through the material will be like hiking on that mountain, living off of it and on it, getting to know its character intimately. Finally, you may decide to make your home there. But bear in mind that the first pass was made quickly, at a distance and without great detail. Every phase of the journey is valuable in its way. Don't denigrate your learning because you're a beginner. Just remember, Rabbi Akiva started learning the *alef-bet* when he was forty years old, and he ended up as one of the greatest sages of all time. You can do it, too. Just don't expect that you're going to grasp all of it all at once.

STUDYING IN PARTNERSHIP

Studying Talmud is not something that's usually done on one's own. Indeed, one of the first rules of Talmud study is the following: "Rabban Gamaliel said: 'Provide yourself with a teacher'" (*Avot* 1:16). Not only should you have one teacher; you should have many teachers over the course of your years (hopefully) of Talmud study:

> "And he shall be like a tree transplanted by streams of water" (Psalm 1:3). Those of the school of R. Jannai said: "a tree *transplanted*," not "a tree *planted*"—[which implies that] whoever learns Torah from one master only will never achieve great success. (*Avodah Zarah* 19a)

As I said before, Talmud study isn't just about learning something intellectually or spiritually; it's about building relationships. And it's about having the right teacher for each stage of your spiritual and intellectual journey. At each phase of your own personal and spiritual progression you'll require different teachers. That doesn't mean the teacher you're leaving wasn't valuable and will not remain in your heart as one of the persons who most benefited you. It just means that there is a time to move on.

What can you expect from a teacher? A teacher should know more about the Talmud, about Judaism, and about spiritual journeys than you do. Any one of these things might not be enough to make a person an appropriate teacher. Then again, only one of these factors might make someone the teacher you need. If you are ready for study, you will find a teacher. God will provide you with that even though you may have to search the teacher out. These days, with the "information superhighway," the teacher might live in another state.

If you keep learning long enough, you will come to a point where you don't need a teacher so much. Then you will be able to use the words of teachers that are written down, either in the traditional commentaries or in modern, scholarly secondary literature, to guide you in your studies. When this starts to happen you will know that it is time to begin to make the transition from the role of student into the role of teacher. Of course, you will always be learning; there's no end to it. So you'll always be a student in some sense, but there's a time to begin teaching as well. That phase can come remarkably quickly as you start teaching what you've learned in casual ways to your children, spouse, or coworkers. Talmud isn't something you just lock up in a compartment in your brain. It affects your whole life.

That's the other thing about Talmud study. If you keep at it long enough, be prepared for your attitude toward God and mitzvot to change. It will gradually become self-evident to you that not keeping kosher, or Shabbat, or the holidays in some form is really absurd. You might not want to change but you won't be able to help it. So if you don't want to change your life, watch out!

SETTING UP AN ENVIRONMENT FOR STUDY

Everyone has different study habits and you will develop your own personal style of study. However, here are some guidelines for establishing an environment that will facilitate your study of Talmud.

1. **Study on a table.** If the table is in a Jewish library, so much the better because you will have to . . .

2. **Get used to having many volumes** of books out at one time. By the end of a study session you could have several books spread out on the table: the volume you are studying, a Bible to look up the verses that are cited in the Talmud, the *Reference Guide* for this set of Talmud, volumes of the *Encyclopaedia Judaica* to provide additional historical background information, various Hebrew or Aramaic dictionaries, and other volumes of rabbinic literature. This isn't messiness. This is the traditional mode of study and it really feels great.

3. **Study out loud.** It helps enormously to read the passage under study out loud, often more than once. Talmud takes patience and repetition and discussion.

4. **Have lots of writing implements at hand.** Writing in the margins is your way of making the Talmud your own, so go ahead

and mark up the text and fill in those blank margins with your own thoughts. Who knows, maybe 1,000 years from now they'll be studying your comments along with Rashi's!

TALMUD STUDY AS A PERSONAL JOURNEY

I have talked a bit already about the spiritual journey of Talmud study. However, we might do well to make this explicit. In each step forward you take there will be a paradox. This is the nature of spiritual development. For example, one of the biggest paradoxes is that you need to have a healthy ego to study Talmud at all. If you are too disturbed, depressed, down on yourself, or the like, you won't be able to fully engage in the process. But as you go along, it will become clear to you that spiritual progress depends on giving up your ego in order to make room for God's will in your life. Similarly, you need some degree of intellect to enter the world of the Talmud. But, as we already mentioned, if this is the only way you understand the Talmud, you will be defeated.

I have gone through many stages in my years of studying Talmud. When I first opened a volume of it as a teenager, I was repulsed. I had scarcely read anything seemingly less connected with my life. When I was in rabbinical school I was similarly put off by Talmud and took only the required courses and did not take one elective in Talmud, per se, although I did study Midrash. It was only after I was a rabbi and I started studying on a daily basis with an Orthodox rabbi that I came to my love of Talmud. After a time, I studied on my own. I became infatuated with the Talmud, one might say. Except for my husband and children, it completely filled me up and suffused my spirit and being. This is a great phase and in a way I'm sorry it's over. I just drank it in and drank it in. But even this phase comes to an end and I began to go at the Talmud with my intellect, this time reading secondary literature and picking up a Ph.D. in Talmud along the way. Now, I feel like I form, with the Talmud, a long-married couple. I know it well but it can still delight and surprise me.

This cycle of going at the Talmud in different ways is not a ladder. It's more like a spiral staircase. You keep reusing approaches you've tried before. You just come back to them at a higher level.

Things that didn't seem interesting to you when you first started will be fascinating later on and vice versa. The same passage you understood one way will strike you differently the second, third, or tenth time you study it. Think of it as visiting a foreign country (albeit one where everyone is a distant relative). If you're a tourist visiting for the first time, you'll likely concentrate on the most pleasant highlights, which are approachable through well-worn paths. If you return, you'll try to make friends, enter people's homes, and find out how they live. Then, you may begin to commute regularly (I would say this is the stage I currently occupy). Finally, you may decide to become a citizen and stay there all the time (one could venture a guess that this is where Rabbi Steinsaltz is). You keep revisiting the old sites—it's just that you have a different appreciation of them. Perhaps it is akin to the different ways a tourist and a Parisian look at the Eiffel Tower. They both think it's great but one can't wait to see it for the first time and the other treats it as a beautiful part of the scenery.

What are some of the phases you are likely to go through? First, there is the curiosity/frustration phase. It's all so darn foreign and hard and you've never read anything like it. Just skimming through the *Reference Guide* can help with this phase. In fact, some students of Talmud I know do just that before they ever look at the text and enjoy themselves for months in this way. This stage resolves as you begin to get familiar with the sages' world.

Often the phase that follows is the anger/rebellion phase because you perceive the Talmud as a source of authority in Judaism that is extremely "politically incorrect." It's best not to become stuck in this phase because it's pretty counterproductive. If you really pay attention to the text, you'll soon realize that, even though Jewish law was deduced, in the main, from the Babylonian Talmud, Jewish law isn't the Talmud's main agenda. In other words, the folks who put the Talmud together were incredibly bright. If they had wanted to compose a book of laws, they could have done so. But that's not what they did. They composed a book that shows you underlying values in decision-making and demonstrates how to think about issues. They appear to have believed that how you thought about issues was at least as important as, if not more important than, the exact decision you came up with. The sages knew that if you have a good decision-making process then, in general, we can trust your decisions.

Another phase is the one where you see the whole thing as a giant jigsaw puzzle and you're interested in how it was put together. This is tremendous fun and can really tickle your brain. Yet another phase is one in which you feel you know the people in the Talmud personally. At this point, just as your friends influence you in life, the sages of the Talmud begin to influence your Jewish and spiritual behavior. You gain a new understanding of the mitzvot. It's not that some external entity is commanding you to observe the mitzvot. They are something you feel compelled to do because of who you have become. In this way, you add mitzvot to your life in a gradual, organic, healthy way that is totally natural and inevitable. Each one you add is like a present you give yourself, and you treasure it and remember when you added it to your life. This may be what the sages themselves are referring to in this passage:

> What is the meaning of the verse, "Wealth gotten by vanity shall be diminished, but he that gathers little by little shall increase"? (Proverbs 13:11)—If one studies by heaps at a time, he will benefit but little, but if one gathers [knowledge] little by little he will gain much. (*Avodah Zarah* 19a)

This brings up another issue. How often should you study? Of course, the sages have some advice on this matter, too:

> Shammai said: Make your study of the Torah a regular habit; say little but do much and receive every person cheerfully. (*Avot* 1:15)

What's regular? That's probably up to you to decide. But you will have to make a steady effort in order to really feel like you're making progress. Every week for several years, or every day for several months, is not unreasonable to attain the goals we have been discussing.

SOME BASIC TERMS

Before you get started, there are some basic terms you'll need to know. Let's put the concepts you'll need to know in modern terms. Imagine that I am an expert on coffee. I have six basic teachings that I am known for:

1. Coffee is good.
2. Coffee should be drunk in the morning.
3. Coffee should be drunk with cream and sugar.
4. Coffee should be drunk in moderation.
5. Always smell the milk before you pour it in the cup.
6. Good decaf is good coffee.

Now let's say an editor is going to compile a slim book about coffee that contains teachings of national experts on coffee. This work is composed at a time of great turmoil in the coffee world and this book is to represent the ideal, simple way of preparing and drinking coffee. This editor looks at all six of my teachings and picks only #1 for her book. Later, someone else compiles a larger book about coffee and picks my teachings #2 and #3 for his volume. That still leaves teachings #4, #5, and #6 out there, not included in anyone's book but known about by the coffee community, so to speak. A good while later, someone is writing an encyclopedic volume about coffee and includes in her volume my teachings #4, #5, and #6. This encyclopedic volume uses as an organizational framework the first, slim volume, which is now a classic. It quotes the teachings listed in that first book, often cites those from the second one, and then examines other teachings not found in either volume.

The first book is like the Mishnah, a short, elegant work of guiding principles. Think of the Mishnah as the sages' answer to Plato's *Republic*: a vision of a completely orderly world composed when the actual world of 200 C.E. was frighteningly chaotic. My teaching #1 (Coffee is good), having been included in this volume, would now be called a *mishnah*. The second volume is like Tosefta, a work composed about 20 years after the Mishnah was completed, that is, in 220 C.E. Tosefta is based on the Mishnah's organizational framework and is four times larger than the Mishnah. My teachings #2 and #3, having been included in this work, are each called a Tosefta. The teachings #4, #5, and #6 are each called a Baraita. If #1, #2, and #3 had not been included in the Mishnah or Tosefta, they would still be called Baraitot, too. A Baraita is just a teaching from the era between 70 and 200 C.E. that wasn't picked to be in the Mishnah or Tosefta but is quoted by the Gemara. The Gemara is like the third volume on coffee.

Mishnah and Gemara together form the Talmud. You might want to repeat that out loud several times because it can really get confusing. Mishnah and Gemara together form the Talmud. Mishnah is short, elegant and idealistic. Gemara is long, often technical, and grounded in real life. Together, they make up the Talmud. This should start to give you an idea as to why Talmud can be so many things to so many people: it contains within itself viewpoints, not simply from one end of the spectrum to the other, but around the surface of a sphere. (Note, as you go along, how often the Gemara will take the Mishnah and humanize it; it will fill in the nuances and realities that the Mishnah leaves out. When you start feeling angry at the Mishnah, many times the Gemara will help you deal with that anger.)

Now, how did my teachings about coffee become known? I wasn't just a maker of coffee; I taught classes on my philosophy of coffee and how to brew it and drink it. Most of my students simply followed my coffee philosophy and recipes by rote. They could repeat them and even use them but did not really think about them very much. A few of my students might really have delved into my teachings, thinking about them, trying to understand them, searching deeply into them to discover the secrets of coffee making and drinking and coming up with modifications of my ideas. The first sort of student is analogous to what, in the Talmud, is called a Tanna (literally, a repeater): a person who repeats Mishnayot and Baraitot but who doesn't really think about them. The second person is like the Ḥakham (literally, a sage or wise one) whose comments on the Mishnah form the basis for the Gemara. A sage who engaged in these activities can also be referred to as an Amora.

These terms Mishnah, Tosefta, Baraita, Gemara, Tanna, Ḥakham, and Amora are terms you should have a working knowledge of before you open a volume of the Steinsaltz. You might want to try role-playing the positions and using the terminology outlined above. You might also want to look them up in the *Reference Guide*, too, before you start.

Now, using the *Reference Guide* can pose a bit of a problem if you don't know Hebrew because it's organized according to the Hebrew alphabet. That being the case, in this volume I'll guide you to the appropriate entries in a way that does not require a knowledge of Hebrew. I'll give you the page number and the column, and I'll count down the number of entries in that column, starting with the first complete entry as number one. So, for example, you can find the terms we've just discussed in the *Reference Guide* at these locations:

Amora: page 104, column 2, 7th entry
Baraita: page 107, column 2, 6th entry
Gemara: page 108, column 2, 4th entry under the letter Gimel
Tanna: page 142, column 2, last entry

THE REAL STORY ON
RITUAL PURITY AND IMPURITY

Another essential thing you'll need to know to understand the Talmud is the real story behind the laws of ritual purity and impurity. First of all, get out of your mind that this has anything to do with dirtiness or negativity. Such concepts result from the inability to accurately translate the words *taharah* (purity) and *tum'ah* (impurity) into English. What this really has to do with is boundaries between life and death and helping us deal with times, places, and things that involve ambiguity in those boundaries.

Think about the following real-life, modern example. A woman's father was in a hospital in the process of dying from cancer. He had to be moved to a new room. The last occupant had died in the room to which he was to be moved. The nurse found this information important enough that she asked the woman if she minded if her father was put in a room in which the last occupant had died. (He later died in that room.) There was probably nothing objective about the room that caused the death. Yet, our intuition tells us that something about the death happening there had changed the room. It is as if, in passing out of this world, a bit of "disembodied soul residue" was left in the room. This feeling, this concept, *this* is what ritual impurity is about. Anything that is connected with death is in some way impure, that is, it is touched with "disembodied soul residue." So, for example, blood that is flowing unstaunchably (e.g., menstrual blood) is considered impure because it is normally related to death: if a wound bleeds uncontrollably, death is the inevitable result. Only whole, complete items (obviously, defined by cultural norms) can become impure. Incomplete or broken items cannot become impure; they cannot receive the "disembodied soul residue." So, for example, a plate of pottery could become ritually impure but the shards of a broken plate of pottery could not.

Paradoxically, touching the Torah can make your hands impure. Why? Because something that is holy has "disembodied soul residue" in it. That's part of what makes it holy. All the people who have reverently read a given Torah scroll leave an essence of their soul in that scroll. You might try opening a Torah scroll to see if you can sense this. This will be especially evident if you can compare an old scroll with a new one. The sensation is indescribable but definitely there. This also hints at a deep mystical truth: the most life-intensifying thing in our faith (Torah) is reminiscent of death, too. (Remember how I said that spiritual development involves paradox? Really living means living now and after you die and understanding how that works. Death doesn't necessarily have to refer only to physical death. It can also denote the death by degrees that comes from not actually living your life.)

You might want to look up these entries in the *Reference Guide*:

Taharah: page 195, column 1, 4th and 5th entries
Tum'ah: the last entry on page 195–page 197, column 2, 2nd
    entry

When you read in the Talmud about ritual purity and impurity, think about it as a discussion of embodiment, the soul, and wholeness rather than as one about dirt or defilement.

TITHES AND LAWS OF JEWISH AGRICULTURE

Another topic that occurs over and over again are the tithes on produce. It's better to figure out how that system works now rather than stumbling on the terms later and becoming frustrated by them.

Let's say you are a farmer in the ancient Land of Israel. Everything you grow and every animal you raise has a relationship with

Judaism. Let's start with animals first. If you owned a flock of animals, one out of every ten animals born during a given period had to be offered up in the Temple. In addition, each firstborn, blemishless male calf, sheep, or goat had to be given to a priest to be offered in the Temple.

If you owned a field, the first fruits of a new harvest were given to priests (about 1/60 of a crop). This gift of first fruits (*bikkurim*) was brought to the Temple on Shavuot in a great ceremony that was much like a parade (think: county fair, but holy). Once your crop was ripe, you would first set aside *terumah*. This was about 1/50 of your crop, which you would give to a priest. The priest and his family could only eat this gift if they were in a ritually pure state, since this food is set aside—holy. Separating off part of the crop as *terumah* is the example, par excellence, of doing something for the sages because you are changing something's state with words and intentions (separation of *terumah* is accomplished with a blessing). In other words, something is *terumah* because a person considers it *terumah*, not because there's anything inherently *terumah*-like about it. Therefore, it all depends on a person's intention and action.

After you separated off *terumah*, then you would take out the tithes, or *ma'aserot*. There are several types of *ma'aserot*. The first is a simple 1/10 of the crop given to the Levites. The second tithe was taken from the crop in the first, second, fourth, and fifth years of the seven-year Sabbatical cycle. This tenth of the crop was set aside to be eaten only in Jerusalem, an ancient way of encouraging tourism to the capital. One could take this second tithe and turn it into cash to be spent in Jerusalem on food. The poor person's tithe (*ma'aser oni*) was set aside in the third and sixth years of the seven-year cycle and were given to the poor. In addition *leket*, that is, at least three stalks that fell together in one place during harvest, had to be left for the poor to glean, as well as forgotten sheaves (*shekhiḥah*), which had to be left for the poor, and the corners of the fields remained unharvested so the poor might gather there (*pe'ah*; about 1/60 of the crop).

In addition to all this, one was to let the land lie fallow in the seventh year of the Sabbatical cycle. Any produce that your land yielded in the seventh year of the Sabbatical year cycle was called *shevi'it* (also called *shemitah*) and was considered ownerless (*hefker*) and was left unguarded in the field. Certain restrictions applied to the sale and use of food that grew, untended, during the Sabbatical year.

For further information, see these entries in the *Reference Guide*:

Bekhor: page 170, column 2, last entry
Bikkurim: page 167, column 2, 5th entry
Hefker: page 14, column 2, 1st entry
Leket: page 209, column 1, 3rd entry
Ma'aserot: page 221, column 2, 3rd entry–page 222, column 1, 2nd entry
Pe'ah: page 243, 1st entry under the letter Pey
Terumah: page 275, column 1, 2nd entry

PRIESTS AND LEVITES IN ANCIENT ISRAEL

Now might also be the time to explain the role of the Priest and the Levite in Jewish life in the days of the Temple. The *Kohanim*, the priests, were descended from Aaron and ran the Temple cult. Only male priests with unblemished lineages and bodies in a state of ritual purity could officiate at the cult sacrificing unblemished animals. Why? Because the perfection of God above had to be mirrored as closely as possible in the Temple below. Of course, this tells us a good bit about what the Jewish conception of perfection was in those days. (An interesting question: what is the physical embodiment of perfection now?)

The *Levi'im* were descendants of Levi, Jacob's son, who helped the priests at the cult and also provided music in the Temple. Being a Priest or a Levite meant that one was a member of an aristocratic family. Today it would be like being a member of the Kennedy clan: it has a certain cachet that opens doors and denotes familial superiority. (And just as with the Kennedys, some members of these priestly and levitical clans lived up to their honorable heritage better than others.)

We can understand the Temple and its personnel in much the same way as we think of hospitals today. A hospital is a place of healing and so was the Temple. Hospital staffs are arranged hierarchically: heads of sections, M.D.s, nurses, technicians, and patients. So the "staff" of the Temple was arranged hierarchically as well. Strict rules regarding cleanliness and purity apply in hospitals, and analogous rules applied in the Temple, too.

For further information, see these entries in the *Reference Guide*:

Kohen and *Kohen Gadol*: page 202, column 2, 4th and 5th entries
Levi: page 208, column 1, 4th entry

As you study the Talmud you will encounter many more interesting and foreign concepts related to Jewish life 2,000 years ago. Part of the fun of Talmud study is exploring these issues and feeling you are becoming an expert in this culture. Enjoy!

HOW TO USE THIS BOOK

This book is meant to be used in conjunction with the Steinsaltz English Talmud. It's like an owner's manual. This book points you to passages in each of Rabbi Steinsaltz's volumes that are relatively more accessible than others. That's not to denigrate passages that weren't selected. It's just to point you toward places where it's easiest to enter. The passages are outlined, with notes designed to aid and encourage you in your study. Each passage is numbered, and suggested courses made up of these numbered passages are provided if you want to approach the material thematically.

Different styles of type are used in this book. Indented paragraphs are usually passages from Torah, Tanakh (the Jewish Bible), Rabbinic literature, or scholarly works. Italicized passages are words of encouragement and ways to help you relate the passages to your own life. "Above and Beyond" sections, set as footnotes, are for those who want additional suggestions and challenges as they learn.

In general, as you are learning, it will help to put the situations you are studying into modern terms if you role-play them out. Imagine actually using the rules you are reading about. Put the situation in your own words. Get up and move around as you discuss and act out the scenarios. Talmud should involve your whole being, including your body!

Use visual aids. If graphs, charts, colored markers, and pictures help you understand the passage, use them. If you are responsible for presenting some material to a class, don't be afraid to use materials to bring the lesson to life. For example, if you're teaching about tithes, bring a big container of berries to class and show what portion of the crop would go for which tithes. You can assign class members to the roles of farmer, *Kohen*, Levite, and so on.

One more note: if you are teaching this material and you have never really taught Talmud before, don't be afraid to say to your class, "I don't know but I'll try to find out." I surely don't know it all, and neither does anyone else I've ever studied with. It'll probably make your class feel better to realize that you're just a few steps ahead of them instead of separated from them by a gulf of knowledge.

The way you use the Steinsaltz Talmud will depend on what kind of learner you are. If you are interested in the Hebrew/ Aramaic language, you'll probably use the Literal Translation most often as it will help you understand the text. If you are more interested in discussing ethics and ideas, you'll probably use the Translation with Commentary. If you are interested mostly in Jewish law, you'll want to take special note of the Halakhah at the bottom of the page. As always, the basic guidelines hold: stick with what interests you until you have a firm enough foothold to branch out into other areas.

HOW THE NUMBERS
AND DIFFICULTY FACTORS WORK

Below, you will find delineated thirty passages from present and forthcoming volumes of *The Talmud: The Steinsaltz Edition*. In each case, where possible, the passage is cited according to its traditional folio number from the Babylonian Talmud (i.e., a page number and an "a" or "b" after it) as well as by page and line number in the Steinsaltz edition. Background information is provided to help make the passage more comprehensible. Each passage is numbered and these numbers are the basis for the course outlines that follow.

Each passage is also rated for difficulty. This is its difficulty factor, abbreviated DF. One is as easy as Talmud gets. Five will be as difficult a passage as is presented in this volume. The difficulty factors are all calculated as first encounters with Talmud. The more you study, the easier it will get. What would have been a 5 when you started may be a 2 or even a 1 after several weeks of study. If you are going at this by yourself, you should probably start with the passages that are rated 1 and work your way up to those rated 5. Think of it as the "difficulty factor" in Olympic diving. After you're done with a passage, you can even imagine what score the judges would have given you!

2

Course Outlines

TALMUD ON A BUDGET: SIX COURSES

These courses need only one volume and the *Reference Guide*. Each selection, or group of selections, is long enough to constitute a class of several weeks in length.

Course 1—No. 12. The Commerce of Perceptions and Feelings, DF = 1

One of the longest passages presented in this volume, it contains the famous story of the conflict between Rabbi Eliezer and the sages over the "oven of Akhnai" issue. It includes a passage about the importance and strength of feelings and how crucial it is not to hurt others emotionally. It also contains a good bit of material about business ethics and honest business practices.

Course 2—No. 15. Suffering and Sages, DF = 2

This passage would be good for a class that wants to explore the question, "What role does pain play in my life?" The sufferings of several sages, and the deeper meaning these sufferings have, are examined in this passage.

Course 3—No. 20. Weddings and Funerals, DF = 5

This would be a good passage for a class that is interested in transitional moments in life and how Judaism deals with them. This

material might be especially nice for support groups for the be-
reaved or parents whose children are becoming *b'nei mitzvah*.

Course 4—No. 30. On the Merits of the Land of Israel and the World to Come, DF = 4

This would be a very nice passage for those who are going to, have
just come back from, or support Israel. Also, those who are interested in the sages' vision of life after death will find this passage
interesting.

Course 5—Nos. 2–10, that is, all the passages from Volume II

These short passages from Volume II together form a nice, several-
week course introducing students to all manner of Talmudic sub-
jects such as Halakhah, Midrash, business ethics, human relationships, and so forth.

Course 6—Nos. 23, 24, and 25, that is, all the passages from Volume X

This could be one of the most interesting courses presented in this
volume. It deals with how to respond to changing times, the roles
men, women, and children play in family life, how often one
should engage in marital relations, and love stories of the sages.

STORIES OF THE SAGES

These passages have more "plot" than the more practical passages
and, in general, are easier. This would be a good introductory
course that can help you familiarize yourself with the sages.

No. 3. A Rabbi's Honesty, DF = 3

This relatively short passage addresses such questions as: Should
rabbis be put up on pedestals? When is it proper for a sage to lie?
What do you do when someone isn't living up to expectations?
Can you jump to conclusions about people?

No. 6. Above the Law, DF = 3

This short passage, which contains an almost slapstick-type comedy scene, also addresses serious issues such as when we should go beyond the letter of the law and how we truly give things up. In addition, this passage contains a nice midrash on the commandments that bring peace between people.

No. 12. The Commerce of Perceptions and Feelings, DF = 1

One of the longest passages presented in this volume, it contains the famous story of the conflict between Rabbi Eliezer and the sages over the "oven of Akhnai" issue. It includes a passage about the importance and strength of feelings and the importance of not hurting others emotionally. It also contains a good bit of material about business ethics and honest business practices.

No. 15. Suffering and Sages, DF = 2

This is one of the longest, if not the longest, passage outlined in this volume. Its main theme is the exploration of the role pain plays in one's life and the way different sages dealt with this issue. Along the way we have some "locker room" material as well as some stories about the power of prayer, Elijah the prophet, and the intense relationship that can develop between teacher and student. You'll really feel as if you know these sages and their personalities by the time you finish with this passage.

No. 19. The Fragrance of the World to Come, DF = 1

This is a very short passage about a sage who speaks with Elijah the prophet about how difficult it is to study Talmud. This beautiful story demonstrates how God provided the means for one sage to study.

No. 25. How Often to Have Sex and Love Stories of the Sages, DF = 3

This is a relatively long passage but basically an easy one. It is all about how often one is obligated to have marital relations and how the sages fulfilled (or did not fulfill) this mitzvah. It includes stories about how some sages, in order to study, stayed away from their wives for many years, including the very famous (and romantic) story of Rabbi Akiva and his wife, Rachel.

No. 27. How to Deal with Persons with a Dread Disease, DF = 2

This passage of medium length has direct relevance today, for it shows us how different sages dealt with a dread, contagious disease. It shows us how to overcome our fears when faced with mortal danger.

No. 28. Dying with Dignity, DF = 2

This passage of medium length tells the beautiful, but heartbreaking, story of Rabbi Yehudah HaNasi's death. It addresses such issues as when to cease care for a terminally ill patient, what happens when one man commits suicide, passing on power and authority from one generation to the next, and the way a humble but pious woman overcame a large group of sages.

MIDRASH AND TORAH INTERPRETATION

This course might be a good one for a Torah study group that wants to branch out into Talmud. If the group is interested in the four-tiered method of Torah study known as *Pardes*, that is, *peshat*, *remez*, *drash*, *sod*, or the simple meaning, the meaning that is hinted at, the level the sages flesh out in the midrash, and the mystical meaning of the Torah, this would be a good introduction to the "*drash*" level. Also, for non-Jews who are interested in Jewish exegesis of the Bible, this would be a good introduction to the subject.

No. 7. The Art of the Drash, DF = 2

A passage of medium length and a great deal of repetition. We are presented here with thirteen examples of a certain grammatical form that occurs frequently in the Torah and the way the sages expounded on this form. This section of the Talmud shows how fanciful the sages could be when interpreting Torah and how much fun they had (and how much fun you can have).

No. 8. Your Parents vs. God, DF = 2

This short passage, which introduces the midrashic technique of exploring why certain Torah verses are put together, poses the following question: "What happens when your loyalty to God and your loyalty to your parents is in conflict?"

No. 13. Everything Is Connected: A Mystical Midrash, DF = 4

This short but relatively difficult passage links several Torah passages together in a way that shows that the Exodus from Egypt, honesty in business practices, and integrity in religious dealings are all related in Jewish life.

No. 17. Concretizing the Spiritual: What Is a Blessing? DF = 1

One of the sages' fascinating tendencies is to take concrete things and make them spiritual and spiritual things and make them concrete. The latter is what they do in this short passage. They take a verse about blessings in Deuteronomy and concretize the definition of a blessing. This passage also contains material about how medicine was practiced in that era, including how important it was to eat breakfast (!).

No. 18. Who Is Needy? DF = 5

This medium-length passage is one that some learners find difficult and others find to be of only moderate difficulty. It is especially interesting for those interested in how the sages reconciled two passages from the Torah that are slightly different. The difference between a person who is destitute and one who is merely needy is explored. It also touches on the importance of prompt payment as a basic precept of Jewish business ethics.

THE WORLD OF THE SAGES:
THE HISTORY/ANTHROPOLOGY OF THAT ERA

This is a course for those who are interested in discovering the world of the sages and the historical realities they dealt with. This course might be good in a secular venue such as a university setting or non-Jewish groups that want to learn about the history of Judaism.

No. 1. Clearing Ancient Credit Reports, DF = 1

This very short selection highlights how different information transmission and record keeping were in the sages' day when compared with our own. So much depended on the testimony of witnesses and their reliability. The absence of copying machines, faxes, and the like affected the way people did business and made one's reputation for truth telling (or lying) extremely important.

No. 2. Losing and Finding, DF = 1

This is one of the shortest and easiest passages presented in this volume, yet it presents some profound issues for consideration. What does it mean to lose something? To find something? What are your obligations if you find something? When does a person give up hope of recovering a lost item?

No. 4. What Is Stealing? DF = 3

This relatively brief passage examines when, exactly, an act of thievery has taken place. This is not as simple a question as it seems. For example, if you see someone drop an item and you pick it up, meaning to return it to him, and then later change your mind and decide to keep the item, is this stealing? When did the stealing take place?

No. 5. Torah Scrolls: A Special Case, DF = 4

Books (which were scrolls in the sages' day) and other holy items that could be lost or stolen are the subject of this short passage.

This is a good passage for those who want to look at how the Talmud is put together, for the different composite materials in this passage are easy to discern.

No. 6. Above the Law, DF = 3

This short passage, which contains an almost slapstick-type comedy scene, also addresses serious issues such as when we should go beyond the letter of the law and how we truly give things up. In addition, this passage contains a nice midrash on the commandments that bring peace between people.

No. 8. Your Parents vs. God, DF = 2

This short passage, which introduces the midrashic technique of exploring why certain Torah verses are put together, poses the following question: "What happens when your loyalty to God and your loyalty to your parents is in conflict?"

No. 9. Teacher as Parent, DF = 2

This passage of medium length brings forth an important Jewish principle: one's teachers are like one's parents and one's students are like one's children. This passage explores this dynamic as well as the definition of the role "teacher." How best to study and what texts of the Jewish tradition one should study and when are also discussed.

No. 16. Spiritualizing the Concrete: What Is a House? DF = 1

This short passage takes a concrete definition of a house (i.e., who is obligated to make repairs, the tenant or the landlord?) and concentrates on its spiritual aspect, the mezuzah placed on the doorway.

No. 21. Truth or Tact? DF = 1

This medium-length passage is one of the most famous in the Talmud. It outlines the dispute between two great schools, those of

Shammai and Hillel, as to how one should praise a bride: with strict accuracy or with greater tact. Songs sung for the ordination of rabbis as well as funeral customs and even a fiery funeral are recounted.

No. 22. "Who Is a Jew?" and "Consequences of Inappropriate Sexual Intercourse," DF = 5

Though this is a short passage, it is one of the most difficult because of the subject matter it addresses. This Mishnah deals with the consequences of rape, divisions within Jewish society, and how restitution for such a crime is to be made. This passage will take time to work through, both in terms of a simple understanding of the material and on the emotional level.

No. 23. A Judaism that Responds to the Times: The Dictates of Usha, DF = 5

How do we cope with a world turned upside down? What turn out to be our most important values in this situation? Raising children with adequate financial support, giving to charity in a reasonable way, and educating children are some of the values the sages canonized in the decisions they laid down in a town called Usha after the destruction of the Temple. This passage of medium length is a good one for those who wish to explore the importance of the family in Judaism.

No. 24. A Wife's Obligations to Her Husband, DF = 2

What jobs did the role "wife" entail for women in the sages' day? This medium-length passage demonstrates that a woman's role was as multifaceted then as now. This is also a great passage for contrasting the theoretical views of the Mishnah with the real-life world of the Gemara. There is interesting information here on breastfeeding practices of ancient times.

No. 25. How Often to Have Sex and Love Stories of the Sages, DF = 3

This lengthy passage is an easy one to understand, containing many stories about the sages' relationships with their wives. What sorts of men are obligated to have sex with what frequency is also outlined here. The very romantic story of Rabbi Akiva and his wife Rachel is contained in this passage.

No. 27. How to Deal with Persons with a Dread Disease, DF = 2

This passage of medium length has direct relevance today, for it shows us how different sages dealt with a dread, contagious disease. It shows us how to overcome our fears when faced with mortal danger.

HOW TO BE A DECENT PERSON: MENSCHLICHKEIT 101

This is a course for those who simply want to study Talmud to help them lead more righteous lives.

No. 3. A Rabbi's Honesty, DF = 3

This relatively short passage addresses such questions as: Should rabbis be put up on pedestals? When is it proper for a sage to lie? What do you do when someone isn't living up to expectations? Can you jump to conclusions about people?

No. 4. What Is Stealing? DF = 3

This relatively brief passage examines when, exactly, an act of thievery has taken place. This is not as simple a question as it seems. For example, if you see someone drop an item and you pick it up, meaning to return it to him, and then later change your mind and decide to keep the item, is this stealing? When did the stealing take place?

No. 6. Above the Law, DF = 3

This short passage, which contains an almost slapstick-type comedy scene, also addresses serious issues such as when we should go beyond the letter of the law and how we truly give things up. In addition, this passage contains a nice midrash on the commandments that bring peace between people.

No. 8. Your Parents vs. God, DF = 2

This short passage, which introduces the midrashic technique of exploring why certain Torah verses are put together, poses the following question: "What happens when your loyalty to God and your loyalty to your parents are in conflict?"

No. 9. Teacher as Parent, DF = 2

This passage of medium length brings forth an important Jewish principle: one's teachers are like one's parents and one's students are like one's children. The passage explores this dynamic as well as the definition of the role "teacher." How best to study and what texts of the Jewish tradition one should study and when are also discussed.

No. 21. Truth or Tact? DF = 1

This medium-length passage is one of the most famous in the Talmud. It outlines the dispute between two great schools, those of Shammai and Hillel, as to how one should praise a bride: with strict accuracy or with greater tact. Songs sung for the ordination of rabbis as well as funeral customs and even a fiery funeral are recounted.

No. 23. A Judaism that Responds to the Times: The Dictates of Usha, DF = 5

How do we cope with a world turned upside down? What turn out to be our most important values in this situation? Raising children with adequate financial support, giving to charity in a reasonable way, and educating children are some of the values the sages canonized in the decisions they laid down in a town called Usha after the destruction of the Temple. This passage of medium length is a good one for those who wish to explore the importance of the family in Judaism.

No. 26. How to Give Charity, DF = 2

This relatively long passage contains many stories detailing the way the sages gave charity. They were extremely careful to maintain the dignity and individuality of those they aided.

No. 27. How to Deal with Persons with a Dread Disease, DF = 2

This passage of medium length has direct relevance today, for it shows us how different sages dealt with a dread, contagious disease. It shows us how to overcome our fears when faced with mortal danger.

No. 28. Dying with Dignity, DF = 2

This passage of medium length tells the beautiful, but heartbreaking, story of Rabbi Yehudah HaNasi's death. It addresses such issues as when to cease care for a terminally ill patient, what happens when one man commits suicide, passing on power and authority from one generation to the next, and the way a humble but pious woman overcame a large group of sages.

No. 29. On the Dangers of Taking Bribes, DF = 3

The sages acted as judges and the importance of performing this role with absolute integrity is brought out in this medium-length passage. Many charming stories are told here of the lengths to which the sages would go to avoid taking anything that could conceivably be thought to be a bribe. The importance of being authentic instead of being popular is also brought out vividly.

A COURSE IN BUSINESS ETHICS

This would make a nice introduction to Talmud for a group that studies together at work.

No. 4. What Is Stealing? DF = 3

This relatively brief passage examines when, exactly, an act of thievery has taken place. This is not as simple a question as it seems. For example, if you see someone drop an item and you pick it up, meaning to return it to him, and then later change your mind and decide to keep the item, is this stealing? When did the stealing take place?

No. 10. Business Advice, DF = 5

This short passage outlines rules for a successful business person to follow in terms of what sorts of investments to make, how to keep assets safe, and how assets that one is obsessive about are not really blessings.

No. 11. What Is Owning? Acquiring? Money? DF = 5

How do we acquire things? When do we actually own something? How were these processes different and similar then compared to today? This short passage outlines the modes of acquisition in the sages' era.

No. 12. The Commerce of Perceptions and Feelings, DF = 1

One of the longest passages presented in this volume, it contains the famous story of the conflict between Rabbi Eliezer and the sages over the "oven of Akhnai" issue. It includes a passage about the importance and strength of feelings and the importance of not hurting others emotionally. It also contains a good bit of material about business ethics and honest business practices.

No. 14. No Insider Trading and Other Rules of Fairness in Finances, DF = 2

This medium-length passage shows to what lengths the sages go in their efforts to make sure business transactions are accomplished with integrity. Even transmitting information out of gratitude for a loan is forbidden.

No. 18. Who Is Needy? DF = 5

This medium-length passage is one that some learners find difficult and others find to be of only moderate difficulty. It is especially interesting for those interested in how the sages reconciled two passages from the Torah that are slightly different, as modern scholars and religious persons also do. The difference between a person who is destitute and one who is merely needy is explored. It also touches on the importance of prompt payment as a basic precept of Jewish business ethics.

No. 29. On the Dangers of Taking Bribes, DF = 3

The sages acted as judges and the importance of performing this role with absolute integrity is brought out in this medium-length passage. Many charming stories are told here of the lengths to which the sages would go to avoid taking anything that could conceivably be thought to be a bribe. The importance of being authentic instead of being popular is also brought out vividly.

A COURSE ON WOMEN

These passages either report rules about women or include women who figure prominently in the stories they contain (although women are rarely the protagonists).

No. 1. Clearing Ancient Credit Reports, DF = 1

This very short selection highlights how different information transmission and record keeping were in the sages' day when compared with our own. So much depended on the testimony of witnesses and their reliability. The absence of copying machines, faxes, and the like affected the way people did business and made one's reputation for truth-telling (or lying) extremely important. A case involving a woman and her father-in-law is presented here.

No. 12. The Commerce of Perceptions and Feelings, DF = 1

One of the longest passages presented in this volume, it contains the famous story of the conflict between Rabbi Eliezer and the sages over the "oven of Akhnai" issue. It includes a passage about the importance and strength of feelings and the importance of not hurting others emotionally. Imma Shalom, Rabbi Eliezer's wife, plays a crucial role in the story, and the husband–wife relationship is explored here.

No. 15. Suffering and Sages, DF = 2

This is one of the longest, if not the longest, passage outlined in this volume. Its main theme is the exploration of the role pain plays in one's life and the way different sages dealt with this issue. Women play prominent roles here and are important symbolically, as well.

No. 17. Concretizing the Spiritual: What Is a Blessing? DF = 1

One of the sages' fascinating tendencies is to take concrete things and make them spiritual and spiritual things and make them concrete. The latter is what they do in this short passage. They take a verse about blessings in Deuteronomy and concretize the definition of a blessing. Women's prayer and righteousness are addressed here. This passage also contains material about how medicine was practiced in that era, including how important it was to eat breakfast (!).

No. 20. Weddings and Funerals, DF = 5

This lengthy passage covers a great deal of interesting material. It outlines the basic structure of the wedding service, how the festive wedding meals were conducted, how the sages thought of Adam and Eve's creation, and how people mourned a death. In addition, we see how relatively spontaneous and fluid prayer and ritual were in the sages' day when compared with our own.

No. 21. Truth or Tact? DF = 1

This medium-length passage is one of the most famous in the Talmud. It outlines the dispute between two great schools, those of Shammai and Hillel, as to how one should praise a bride: with strict accuracy or with greater tact. Songs sung for the ordination of rabbis as well as funeral customs and even a fiery funeral are recounted.

No. 22. "Who Is a Jew" and "Consequences of Inappropriate Sexual Intercourse," DF = 5

Though this is a short passage, it is one of the most difficult because of the subject matter it addresses. This Mishnah deals with the consequences of rape, divisions within Jewish society, and how restitution for such a crime is to be made. This passage will take time to work through, both in terms of a simple understanding of the material and on the emotional level.

No. 23. A Judaism that Responds to the Times: The Dictates of Usha, DF = 5

How do we cope with a world turned upside down? What turn out to be our most important values? Raising children with adequate financial support, giving to charity in a reasonable way, and educating children are some of the values the sages canonized in the decisions they laid down in a town called Usha after the destruction of the Temple. This passage of medium length is a good one for those who wish to explore the importance of the family in Judaism. Examples of case law involving women as well as the teachings of a woman expert in medicine are presented.

No. 24. A Wife's Obligations to Her Husband, DF = 2

What jobs did the role "wife" entail for women in the sages' day? This medium-length passage demonstrates that a woman's role was as multifaceted then as now. This is also a great passage for contrasting the theoretical views of the Mishnah with the real-life world of the Gemara. There is interesting information here on breastfeeding practices of ancient times.

No. 25. How Often to Have Sex and Love Stories of the Sages, DF = 3

This lengthy passage is an easy one to understand, containing many stories about the sages' relationships with their wives. What sorts of men are obligated to have sex with what frequency is also outlined here. The very romantic story of Rabbi Akiva and his wife Rachel is contained in this passage.

No. 26. How to Give Charity, DF = 2

This relatively long passage contains many stories detailing the way the sages gave charity. They were extremely careful to maintain the dignity and individuality of those they aided. The meritorious way Mar Ukba's wife gave charity is told here.

No. 28. Dying with Dignity, DF = 2

This passage of medium length tells the beautiful, but heartbreaking, story of Rabbi Yehudah HaNasi's death. It addresses such issues as when to cease care for a terminally ill patient, what happens when one man commits suicide, passing on power and authority from one generation to the next, and the way a humble but pious woman overcame a large group of sages.

BY VOLUME

Volume I: 1
Volume II: 2, 3, 4, 5, 6, 7, 8, 9, 10
Volume III: 11, 12
Volume IV: 13, 14
Volume V: 15
Volume VI: 16, 17, 18, 19
Volume VII: 20
Volume VIII: 21
Volume IX: 22
Volume X: 23, 24, 25
Forthcoming Volumes: 26, 27, 28, 29, 30

BY DIFFICULTY FACTOR

Factor 1: 1, 2, 12, 16, 17, 19, 21
Factor 2: 7, 8, 9, 14, 15, 24, 26, 27, 28
Factor 3: 3, 4, 6, 25, 29
Factor 4: 5, 13, 30
Factor 5: 10, 11, 18, 20, 22, 23

3

The Passages

1. CLEARING ANCIENT CREDIT REPORTS

Bava Metzia 12b and 17a
Volume I, page 146, lines 3–9, and page 202, lines 4–10
Difficulty Factor: 1

*This is a short, easy passage—some theory and one example of
the law in action—on a topic with which almost all of us have
experience: figuring out snarl-ups in our financial papers and
agreements.*

Today, when credit reports and loan information are all com-
puterized, it is nonetheless quite difficult to maintain accurate
financial records. Correcting mistakes in these records is difficult
and occasionally maddening. Just imagine how it must have been
in ancient days when everything depended on the word of witnesses to a transaction and on a document that might be lost and
later found.

Before reading this Mishnah and just one comment on it from
the Gemara, look up the following entry in the *Reference Guide*:

Shtar: page 264, column 2, 3rd entry.[1]

---

1. The four entries that follow this one might also be of interest to you as
well as the description and drawing of a *shtar get m'kushar* on page 175, column 2, 4th entry.

To understand our Mishnah, think of the following scenario (this process may be aided by class members taking the various roles and acting them out):

1. You, A, mortgage your house, 111 Bet Shammai Drive, in order to obtain a loan from B, the lender.
2. You, A, sell your house to C.
3. You, A, lose the loan document obtained from B.
4. D finds it and turns it into the Court.
5. The Court, reading the note and finding that 111 Bet Shammai Drive is mortgaged, makes C pay back the loan to B.

According to the Mishnah, D should not return the document to the Court because then C might erroneously be made to pay off the loan and, in fact, the Court worries that A and B have colluded to make C pay the loan off. This Mishnah brings up the issue of honesty and money, two categories that, sadly, often are opposed.

An interesting example of these rules in practice is brought on page 202, lines 4–10.[2] This case brings out how important it is, in financial matters, to consistently tell the truth. A single slip, and one is considered a liar, at least in regard to the specific matter at hand. Note how different this is from the way truth-telling is regarded when we are praising a bride (*Ketubot* 16b–17b, Volume VIII, p. 27, line 8–p. 36, line 3). Imagine what sorts of characters were involved in this dispute. Where is Shabbetai's son in this exchange? Why did he agree to let his father be responsible for this? How did the *ketubah* become lost and why? How must the daughter-in-law have felt when Shabbetai denied he ever made the gift? Under what circumstances do financial gifts and obligations strengthen or weaken family ties? Obviously, we can never definitively know the answers to these questions. However, the information we do have would make the basis for a really great short story, in other words, a modern midrash.

What follow are some short segments from Volume Two of *Bava Metzia* that will give us glimpses into life during the Rabbinic era as well as some practice with the sages' method of mid-

---

2. See the description of a *ketubah* in the *Reference Guide*, page 206, column 2, 2nd entry and/or the material under passage No. 20: Weddings and Funerals, in this volume.

rash, that is, exploring a Biblical text. We will not be following the Talmudic arguments through these passages but rather will look at small snapshots of life and thought in those days as recorded in the Talmud.

2. LOSING AND FINDING

Bava Metzia 21a–b
Volume II, page 3, line 1–page 4, line 4
Difficulty Factor: 1

Ethics is not a separate subject for the sages of the Talmud, as if, in any situation, you could open a book, look under a chapter heading, and find the right solution to every problem. Rather, it's a process of balancing competing values until a solution is reached, wherein the greatest amount of values is preserved. While ethical dilemmas may be dramatic, life-and-death decisions, more often they involve the small, everyday events of our lives, such as finding a lost object and how we deal with it. Practicing the "ethical process" in such situations prepares us for the big decision-making moments. That's what this passage is about.

What is losing and finding? This is not such an easy question to answer. For the sages of the Talmud, an item is only lost as long as the original owner is still looking for it. If the owner has given up hope, then the item is no longer considered "lost" and the finder may treat it differently. These problems are introduced in the Introduction to Chapter Two, pages 1–2, which you should read before proceeding. Also, look up the following terms in the *Reference Guide*:

Hefker: page 184, column 2, 1st entry
Shevi'it: page 260, column 2, last entry
Ye'ush: page 198, column 1, 1st entry under the letter Yud

Or you can read about them as described here. *Hefker* is what an object becomes when you completely give up ownership of it. Let's say you're traveling in another city and you leave your umbrella in a cab. You don't remember the cab number or even the cab company. You don't even think about the umbrella until you leave the airport in your hometown and realize you left the umbrella in the cab. At this point, you will likely give up hope of ever retrieving that umbrella. This umbrella is now *hefker*, ownerless. Note that being ownerless depends on the owner's state of mind. This mental turning point of giving up hope of finding something is called *ye'ush*, despair. If you were particularly attached to that umbrella and tried to trace your steps back in order to retrieve it, then it wouldn't be ownerless, *hefker*.

Now, what happens if (God forbid!) someone steals something from you, say a guitar. You make your police report but you eventually quit searching and give up hope of recovering the guitar. Some time goes by and you see that an acquaintance is playing your guitar! You ask where he got that guitar and he tells you he bought it at a pawn shop. It turns out your stolen guitar was "fenced" through that pawn shop. Does your friend have to return the guitar to you? No, because you despaired of finding it (*ye'ush*) and that meant the thief acquired it and your acquaintance legally acquired the guitar. The thief, however, traced through the pawn shop, is obligated under Jewish law to reimburse you for your guitar.

Attitudes toward physical objects and possessions then were somewhat different than they are today. Now we have many (often, too many) things and may not form terribly strong attachments to them because we have so many possessions or can so easily replace possessions. This was generally not the case in the sages' days: one parted with objects unwillingly. Ownership is a matter, not just of physicality or legality but of emotions, of holding on to objects.

The Mishnah on page 3, line 1–page 4, line 4 outlines which objects, if found, must be "announced." If we were formulating this Mishnah today, we would indicate for which objects, if found, you are required to put up posters in your neighborhood announcing that you found them or to take out an ad in the classified section of your newspaper. As you'll see, the Mishnah's basic criterion is that if the item is produced on an "assembly line" basis, so to speak, the owner will despair of recovering it right away. For example, if you lost a can of beans in a supermarket parking lot, there would be no way to differentiate your can of beans from anyone else's. Someone finding it in the parking lot would not be obligated to stand there and shout, "Did someone lose this can of beans?" However, if your can of beans had a certain identifiable dent in it, then you could expect to retrieve it and someone finding that dented can of beans would be obligated to shout about it in the parking lot before taking it.[3]

3. A RABBI'S HONESTY

Bava Metzia 23b–24a
Volume II, page 48, line 1–page 50, line 4
Difficulty Factor: 3

Telling the truth is important . . . but it's not the only important thing or sometimes even the most important thing. This passage shows how the sages balanced the need to tell the truth with the need to be tactful. If you feel this conflict of values occasionally, this passage will be relevant to your life. This passage will also be interesting to those who believe in, let us say, aggressive law-enforcement techniques. Curiosity tickled? Read on.

Should rabbis be put up on pedestals? Should they be held to higher ethical standards than anyone else? The answer given in this passage is Yes and No. Sages were expected to be more honest than the average person, and this passage explores how that expectation affects returning lost items to a sage. It will help you understand this passage if you first read the Background and Notes entries on page 49.

Let's introduce this passage with the following example: Let's say a rabbi today lost a set of tefillin. Since, except for size, all sets of tefillin are pretty much identical, how could the rabbi know if a set of tefillin recovered are his lost ones? If he'd used them for quite some time, they might have a distinctive feature in them that the rabbi could use to identify the tefillin as his own. However, let's

---

3. You might want to leaf through the pages that follow this Mishnah and read some of the marginal notes to get a flavor of life in ancient days. For instance, the entries on pages 10, 11, 13, 14, 23, 34, 43, 44–45, 46, and 47–48 under Background and page 33 under Realia are quite interesting. These will give you a bit of historical background about everyday items in the days of the Talmud and will help you understand the next passage.

say the tefillin were brand new and were lost in a pile of tefillin. In this case, even if the rabbi can identify his own tefillin, we do not return them to him because he could be making a mistake.

On page 49 we learn that sages do, out of modesty, habitually lie about three things. Are there things polite persons lie about today? Truth-telling is important, but it is not the only important value. Not bragging, being discreet about one's sexuality, and not burdening a generous host are also important values, as this passage brings out. Even today, a family that does not want to have its generosity taken advantage of may make an anonymous charitable donation rather than having it publicized abroad. Note how different views are preserved in the Gemara: scholars are accorded some leeway, but if they prove dishonest they are to be treated no differently than the average person.

The story about the dishonest rabbinical student evokes a larger question: what cues do people give us about themselves from which we can draw larger conclusions? Is it proper or fair to "trust your gut instinct" about people without waiting to see if they actually fulfill those expectations? And under what circumstances should we take the law into our own hands, as Mar Zutra did? Did Mar Zutra know something about this student that made him act in this way? Had the student been in trouble before, and that caused Mar Zutra to suspect him? We should also remember that in those days a cloak could be one of the few pieces of property a person might own, and it might have been considered quite precious to a person. Likewise, cloaks could have symbolic significance (e.g., leaders wore special sorts of cloaks), and this may have been a factor in this story. The Notes here show how the later commentators struggled with this issue.[4]

---

4. This passage might lead you to a discussion of the rabbi as role model and whether today a rabbi is held to higher standards than the average person. As you'll see after reading through the passage, we can return lost articles to a rabbi if our experience of that rabbi is one of basic honesty. However, if we know that the rabbi has lied about some things in the past that weren't issues of modesty or common courtesy, then we do not return the items. Here we have to delicately balance our personal knowledge of a given person's honesty and making an exception to a rule that everyone else has to follow. It is faintly reminiscent of members of Congress exempting themselves from the very laws they make. And if the story on page 50 is true, then, just as some U.S. representatives are honest and some are on the take, we can see that some sages were honest and some were not. This should not surprise us.

4. What Is Stealing?

Bava Metzia 26b
Volume II, page 89, line 8–page 92, line 4
Difficulty Factor: 3

This passage has a good bit of theory in it. This is one of those passages that's going to demand that you think logically and analytically and not with your emotions. You might feel uncomfortable reading this passage because some of what it says won't correspond with what you may think is right (just like American law). Remember, (1) the sages could only legislate minimum desired behavior in a way that was logically consistent within the system they constructed. (2) Be sure to analyze statements that upset you in terms of their genre. Are they hypothetical situations or real cases of law with real litigants? If they are the former, just think of some of the wild things you say in class as you tease out the philosophical implications of what you're studying. If someone took those statements out of context, they might appear strange, too.

Before reading this passage, you might want to do the following:

1. **Read the Background material** in the margins.

2. **Review the Biblical verses** on page 1 of this volume and Leviticus 5:20–24:

> And the Lord spoke unto Moses, saying: If anyone sin, and commit a trespass against the Lord, and deal falsely with his neighbor in a matter of deposit or of pledge or of robbery or have oppressed his neighbor, or have found that which was lost, and deal falsely therein, and swear to a lie; in any of all these that a man does, sinning therein; then it shall be if he has sinned and is guilty, that he shall restore that which he took by robbery, or the thing that he has gotten by oppression, or the deposit that was deposited with him, or the lost thing that he found, or any thing about which he has sworn falsely; he shall even restore it in full and shall add the fifth part more thereto; unto him to whom it appertains shall he give it, in the day of his being guilty. (Leviticus 5:20–24)

3. **Read the information** in the *Reference Guide* on Coins, pages 290–293. It is not necessary to learn every detail, just the rough outline of the information.

The categorization of mitzvot into positive and negative commandments, that is, things one must do or must not do, as well as time-bound and not-time-bound commandments, is brought up in this passage. For example, a positive, time-bound commandment is the eating of matzah at the seder: it is something that is to be done and is to be done at a specific time. An example of a positive commandment with no time limit is "honor your father and your mother": it is something that is to be done at all times. A negative, time-bound commandment is fasting on Yom Kippur. An example of a negative commandment with no time limit is the prohibition against adultery, which is to be observed at all times.

The passage breaks down stealing into several separate transgressions of different positive and negative commandments. Motive and timing are crucial to the definition of an act as stealing. For example, is it stealing if you mean to return something to someone but never get around to it? By correlating each component act of thievery with a Biblical precept, Rava explores the nature of stealing. It might help you to use a chart with the different Biblical precepts on one axis and the three scenarios on the other, in order to visualize this intricate scheme. Check those that apply. How much should motive matter? That is the key question underlying this passage. And how do we know that someone has really given up hope? When he or she goes back, looks, searches, and gives up? When one feels in his or her pocket for the coin, realizes it's gone, and decides not to go back and search for it? And how does the person who pocketed the coin know

	Violated			
	Lev. 19:13	Deut. 22:1	Deut. 22:3	Lev. 5:23
1. Saw it fall, picked it up before owner gave up hope, and intended to rob				
2. Intended to return it but changed mind				
3. Picked it up after owner gave up hope				

when the loser of the coin has given up hope? What criteria would you mandate for these categories?[5]

5. TORAH SCROLLS: A SPECIAL CASE

Bava Metzia **29b**
Volume II, page 135, line 6–page 140, line 7
Difficulty Factor: 4

> *Lay in some patience for yourself. It's likely that you'll have to chew this passage over a while to understand how all the pieces come together. What if it's too frustrating trying to keep all the sources and their opinions straight? Don't worry about it! You'll surely grasp the main concept that great care was taken with scrolls and that people learned from them intensely . . . so intensely, in fact, that they might have damaged them in the course of study. You can always come back to this passage when you feel more confident. This is pretty tough material, so you should definitely feel okay about delving into it as deeply as you can and stopping when you become too frustrated.*

The Gemara is a document by scholars, for scholars, and often about scholars. (That doesn't mean you have to be a scholar to study it, though.) Those things that touched these scholars' lives were often examined closely. For example, in this Mishnah and the Gemara to it, the treatment of found and borrowed scrolls is examined. Before you begin to read this passage, you might want to outline in your mind how finding and borrowing are similar and different. Our Mishnah deals with finding, and in the passage a Baraita deals with borrowing (see the *Reference Guide*,

---

5. You might want to share stories of times you have lost and found items and what you did to recover them or return them. What does American law have to say about your situation? (You might want to have a lawyer or judge study this passage with you so that you can contrast what it says with American law.) These are surprisingly important issues in life. Sometimes we get so caught up in the huge, dramatic moral dilemmas of society that we forget that righteous behavior in something as small as returning lost property is an important moral stand.

p. 107, column 2, 6th entry, or the discussion of coffee in the Introduction).[6]

What might bother you in this passage? The statement on page 136, line 5 that exempts a person from carrying something that reduces his dignity might be upsetting. In general, Rabbinic literature is democratic. For example, the House of Hillel's rulings are law and they generally represent the views of the poorer classes. But, as we have often noted, values are held in a balance in Rabbinic literature. Here, a person's dignity overrides the requirement to do a certain mitzvah. For example, what if you found a copy of *Playboy* in a supermarket parking lot? Theoretically, you ought to pick it up and try to find its owner. However, it would probably embarrass most of us to be seen carting around a copy of *Playboy* and so the Mishnah gives us an exemption in such a case as this. This one line is a good example of why you might want to read the Translation and Commentary *and* the Literal Translation. As he often does, Rabbi Steinsaltz has incorporated Rashi's comments into his Translation and Commentary. When you read the Literal Translation here, you see that the Mishnah does not refer to social standing at all but merely to what one is used to doing, rich or poor.

Have you ever had a Torah scroll in your possession or been responsible for one? What rules did you follow? How did having a Torah scroll in your house make you feel? Can we presume, as is questioned on page 138, that a Torah scroll is different from any other object and that you'd be happy if people who found it or borrowed it were using it to study? Today, when Torah scrolls

---

6. If you have access to the Soncino translation of the Talmud, you can find this Baraita in the volume of Minor Tractates, *Masekhet Sofrim*, chapter 5, law #16. This corresponds to the material found in the Steinsaltz translation, page 137, lines 6–13. If you have that volume, you might also want to look at *Masekhet Tefillin*, which outlines the laws of tefillin, especially 1:13, which shows that at one time tefillin did not all look alike, as stated in the Gemara (Steinsaltz, pp. 136–137). Today, the only variation in tefillin is their size. They are all black, cube-shaped, and made of leather. You might want to look at a set of tefillin, especially some that have been opened, and compare them with the writing in a Torah scroll or scroll of Esther. If you were designing tefillin today, given all the technologies we have that the sages did not, how would you arrange to have verses from the Torah attached to your head and arm?

are easily, if not inexpensively, available, should we treat them the way the Gemara says we should treat tefillin? Or does each Torah scroll have a history and character that is distinctive?

Note how the Gemara examines each phrase of the Baraita as thoroughly as it would a Mishnah (pp. 138–140). Using colored markers, you might want to differentiate the sources in this passage so that you can see the organization of it better. You'll need separate colors for Mishnah, Baraita, Tosefta, and Gemara on Mishnah and Gemara on Tosefta. As you'll see, there isn't much direct commentary on the Mishnah at all here, but the Gemara is concentrating on the Baraita instead. This is not uncommon and does not mean that the Mishnah is unimportant but that the Baraita or Tosefta may flesh the Mishnah out and provide a broader base for discussion. Note how important intention is on page 139, lines 6–7. The exact same action could be permitted—even obligatory—or forbidden, depending on the motivation of the person performing the action. Motivations are *real* in Judaism.

This passage is rather difficult because we are juggling so many different sources that make fine distinctions about the use of Torah scrolls. Why do we have so many traditions on this subject? Because this was an important topic for the sages. The treatment of scrolls was central to their scholarly enterprise. Today, it would be similar to "computer nerds" talking in detail about the use of computers, programs, bootleg programs they'd found or borrowed, and the like. It should be clear, though, that the preservation of the scroll is paramount in all these rulings.

Outline for yourself the answers to the following questions for each of the sources in our passage.

1. Mishnah (p. 135, lines 6–9)
    Lost, borrowed, or deposited?
    Read or roll how often?
    Allowed to learn for the first time from this scroll?
    Allowed to learn with someone else from this scroll?
2. Baraita, First Case (p. 137, lines 6–8)
    Lost, borrowed, or deposited?
    Read or roll how often?
    Allowed to learn for the first time from this scroll?
    Allowed to learn with someone else from this scroll?

3. Baraita, Second Case (p. 137, lines 9–13)
   Lost, borrowed, or deposited?
   Read or roll how often?
   "The First Tanna" (i.e., the Baraita itself)
   Summakhos' opinion
   Rabbi Eliezer ben Yaakov's opinion
   Allowed to learn for the first time from this scroll?
   Allowed to learn with someone else from this scroll?

Perhaps one of the most confusing parts of all these sources that are woven together are the prohibitions against learning something for the first time. This is actually logical. Just think of the difference in the way you read a novel and the way you read a textbook in preparation for an examination. You breeze through the novel, scarcely touching it. However, you underline and make notes in the textbook and go over and over passages as you study. Now imagine that two people were trying to prepare for an exam using the same textbook. In no time at all you'd be fighting over which page to read, and it's easy to see how the book might become damaged or overused in such a way. This is why the Mishnah prohibits a person from learning something new from a lost scroll and from learning from such a scroll by more than one person.

Another issue that might be confusing in this passage is the concept, contrasted with the cases of tefillin and scrolls, that someone wants a mitzvah performed with his or her lost items. We can think of it in the following modern terms: Let's say you were moving cross country, and in the process you lost a run-of-the-mill kiddush cup and brass Shabbat candlesticks that had been in your family for generations. Now let's say that someone found these items and it is some time before they can be returned to you. How do you feel about the person using your kiddush cup for Shabbat? You'd probably feel good about it because at least the cup is being used for a mitzvah. The cup has no special meaning to you and you are glad it is being used appropriately until it can be returned to you. However, you'll feel differently about the candlesticks. You would probably want the person who found them to keep them polished, but you might want that person to put them away lest they be damaged rather than using them every Friday night. This is very much like the difference between tefillin and scrolls as outlined in this passage. One is a standard object that the owner presumably wants to be used for a mitzvah while the other is individual and precious and the owner would want it guarded more than used.

6. ABOVE THE LAW

Bava Metzia 30b
Volume II, page 152, line 1–page 155, line 10
Difficulty Factor: 3

> *You need some technical knowledge about ownerless property to understand this passage (don't worry—it's described here). This passage is funny and meaningful, and it reminds you how to relate to others through mitzvot.*

Before you read this passage, you might want to do the following things.

1. **Refresh your memory** of Exodus 23:5 and Deuteronomy 22:4 by rereading them on page 1 in the Introduction.

2. **Look up these terms** in the *Reference Guide* or see above, the Introduction, and passage #5, where these terms are explained:

> *Hefker*: page 184, column 2, 1st entry
> *Shevi'it*: page 260, column 2, last entry

3. **Refresh your memory** of the section of the Mishnah on which this passage is based (p. 136, line 5).

As we already mentioned, special rules applied to the sages. Since the Talmud is a document written by, for, and about sages, these rules—and cases involving these rules—are documented in detail. In this passage, we have a case of a sage who is aware of the commandment to help unload and load another's burden and yet feels that the honor of the sages would be diminished by fulfilling this mitzvah. (This story—p. 152, lines 3–11—is a fine example of humor in the Talmud! It could be a slapstick routine in a movie.) The sages' note on the side of pages 152–153 is important here because we learn that Rabbi Yishmael was not only brilliant but wealthy.

The Gemara goes on to seriously consider this story on page 153. It explores the following issue: what does it mean to really give something up, to truly renounce ownership of something? If you are really renouncing it, then it has to be unconditional or there is still some tie between you and the object. The example par excellence of renouncing ownership is shemitah or shevi'it: the fruits of the seventh year are completely ownerless. Why does it make sense for Bet Shammai, which represents rich Jews, to take the view that you can renounce property to poor persons but not to rich ones? It is similar to a well-off person who gives furniture or clothing away to charity or a resale shop that serves only indigent clientele. Bet Hillel, representing the lower classes, makes no such distinction: you either own an object or you do not.

An extremely important concept is introduced on page 154: going beyond the requirements of the law (under Concepts). Law can only mandate the minimum required behavior. Therefore, it stands to reason that there is behavior that is desirable that is above the law, and this is what our passage is all about. In this connection, the Gemara brings a beautiful Midrash.[7] This is just one example of the way the sages could take a text from the Torah and make it relevant to their lives (the Background note on p. 154 is especially helpful in spelling out how they related each phrase to each specific mitzvah). If you were to make your own Midrash on each part of this verse, Exodus 18:20, what would it be? The passage then goes on to explore the importance of going beyond the letter of the law (p. 155) and mentions that Jerusalem was destroyed because people insisted on their full rights.[8]

The discussion about visiting the sick on the top of page 155 points to some very important truths. First, there is an obligation to visit the sick even if this represents a slight danger to the visitor. Second, one who visits the sick takes away some of their burden of loneliness and pain. We can experience this viscerally when

---

7. The Baraita can be found in Lauterbach's *Mekhilta d'Rabbi Yishmael*, volume 2, Yitro, chapter 2, pp. 182–183, or in the Hebrew (p. 198, lines 3–13) (Jerusalem: Wahrmann Books, 1970). This is an early Midrash on the Book of Exodus.

8. There are many interesting illustrations of this idea and stories about the destruction of Jerusalem in *Gittin* 55b–58a that are easily understandable when read in English. If you want to progress past Rabbi Steinsaltz's translation, this would be a good place to start. It takes a great historical event and cleverly relates it to the way average people behaved.

we visit the sick: often we leave feeling somewhat saddened and more aware of human frailty, while the person we visited feels partially restored in his or her humanity, which the process of illness can strip away. Thus, we take away a bit, one-sixtieth, of their illness.[9]

7. THE ART OF THE DRASH

Bava Metzia 31a–b
Volume II, page 162, line 5–page 173, line 1
Difficulty Factor: 2

This is a passage designed to make you feel competent quickly! It is thirteen examples of one rather easily comprehended phenomenon. You'll feel like an old hand at the method by the time you're done. Enjoy!

We have not really explored the way the Talmud was put together. However, this is one of the most fascinating topics in all of Talmud study. Naturally, many scholarly volumes have been written on the topic and we do not intend to explore the myriad theories they propound. However, in this passage, we will see one example of the end product of Talmudic development. It begins when

---

9. There is a long discussion of the rules relating to visiting the sick on *Nedarim* 39a–41b. If you are interested in this topic, you might want to look at this passage. Herewith is provided "one-sixtieth" of this delightful material:

Seven things were created before the world: the Torah, repentance, the Garden of Eden, Gehenna, the Throne of Glory, the Temple and the name of the Messiah. . . .

R. Helbo fell ill. Thereupon R. Kahana went and proclaimed: R. Helbo is sick. But none visited him. He rebuked them [the sages] saying, "Did it not once happen that one of Rabbi Akiva's disciples fell sick, and the Sages did not visit him? So Rabbi Akiva himself entered [his house] to visit him, and because they swept and sprinkled the ground before him, he recovered. Said he, "My master, you have revived me." [Straightaway] Rabbi Akiva went forth and lectured: He who does not visit the sick is like a shedder of blood. . . .

He who visits the sick will be delivered from the punishments of Gehenna. . . .

Abaye said: We have it on tradition that no one is poor save he who lacks knowledge. In the West [the Land of Israel] there is a proverb: He who has this, has everything; he who lacks this, what has he? Has one acquired this, what does he lack? Has he not acquired this, what does he possess? (*Nedarim* 39b–41a)

one sort of story or, in this case, Midrash, is brought and then—as if footnotes were added right into the text itself—other examples of the same phenomenon are added into the passage, even though they do not bear directly on the subject at hand. You could almost think of it as similar to the formation of a pearl: it starts with one grain of an idea and then gradually develops over time.

This is a series of thirteen examples of the same phenomenon. Each starts with the premise that not one word of the Torah is superfluous. Therefore, if a word seems superfluous, it must have a hidden meaning that should be explored. One feature of Biblical Hebrew lends itself to this technique. It is called the *makor* form and is a way of saying something with intensity—a kind of italics, as it were. This *makor* form is the same verb in two different forms together. If it were translated literally, it would be, "opening, you shall open" or "returning, you shall return." What this form actually means is "you should absolutely open" or "you must surely return." It is quite common in the Torah text. However, we can see how easy it would be to interpret each part of this verb form separately, and that's just what the sages do.

Here is an example of the sages' playfulness. The way they fondly turn each word over and over is reminiscent of a mother with her infant, listening to every coo intently and kissing the baby over and over. It is a moment of love and play and joy. That's part of what the sages are giving expression to here: their love of Torah. However, they are also discerning serious messages from the text with this method. Go ahead and smile if this material makes you feel happy or amused—it's okay!

Once you get the hang of this type of Midrash, you'll be able to work your way through this passage easily and even attempt to develop your own Midrashim in this way. It may help you to have a Bible handy to look up these verses in context. If you can read Hebrew, having the Hebrew on hand will also be helpful. On page 165 an interesting topic is introduced: the value of rebuking someone, even someone senior to you in virtue and learning. The Halakhah (pp. 165–166) on this matter has some helpful guidelines about how this is best, and most tactfully, accomplished. The examples on pages 170–171 about giving charity are particularly beautiful, as well.

On page 172, line 1, and particularly the Concepts entry on that page, and in the Notes on page 173, those who have not been charmed by this Midrashic technique will find their compatriots in Jewish tradition. Diversity within Jewish intellectual thought is natural and desirable. One school, Rabbi Akiva's, taught that these double forms were to be explored as they have been in the Gemara. Another school, Rabbi Ishmael's, said, "No. These double verb forms are just intense forms and do not have these double meanings." This division between imaginative and rationalistic, and the inclusion of both viewpoints (even though the imaginative one is given more space here), is characteristic of the Gemara. When presented with a choice between two viewpoints, the Gemara often chooses both and validates both as legitimate Jewish responses to a question.[10]

8. YOUR PARENTS VS. GOD

Bava Metzia 32a
Volume II, page 179, line 6–p. 181, line 4
Difficulty Factor: 2

> *The Talmud teaches us to hold our values in balanced proportion to each other. So what happens when two very important values are in conflict? This passage shows how the Talmud deals with such a conflict.*

This passage introduces another often-used Midrashic technique: exploring the juxtaposition of clauses in one verse to bring out a basic truth. In Leviticus 19:3, the obligation to honor par-

---

10. If you want to try this method on a verse not presented in this passage, try looking at Psalm 126:6 (the one we sing before the Grace after Meals on Shabbat):

He who goes (*halokh yeileikh*) and crying, carrying a bag of seeds, shall come (*bo yavo*) in joy carrying his sheaves.

What could each part of the double forms mean? Could they simply mean that one goes continually and returns continually? Or could they refer to this world and the World to Come? Why would someone cry when sowing seeds? Here is your chance to try the method you learned in this passage.

ents and the obligation to honor God are juxtaposed. But what if honoring your parent would involve disobeying God? Should you still honor your parent or should you disregard his or her orders? This passage explores the issue by introducing the question of a priest's father who orders the priest to enter a cemetery and thereby become ritually impure. Priests are not permitted to become ritually impure by entering a cemetery unless they are mourning their relatives because it would impair their ability to function at the cult.

The issue of ritual impurity is often emotionally charged today, and it shouldn't be. The rules regarding ritual impurity have to do with the sages' love of life and fear of death. Menstrual blood was deemed impure not because a menstruating woman was dirty in any way but rather because it was connected with death in two ways. First, any flow of blood that could not be stopped was associated with death as, indeed, such blood flowing from a wound would in fact be. Second, the sages knew that a menstrual flow meant there was no pregnancy and this, too, was associated with a lack of life, if not death itself. Priests, who had to function in a state of ritual purity, had to stay separate from death and everything associated with it. Therefore, a priest was forbidden to enter a cemetery. Even today, in Jerusalem, there are road signs directing priests to a different route rather than driving through the cemetery on the Mount of Olives.

Today the issue of respecting one's parents and being true to one's practice of Judaism is most critical when a child has grown to be more Jewishly observant than the parent. For example, should you drive on Shabbat to the geriatric center where your parent resides? Should you refuse to eat in your parents' house because they don't keep kosher and you do? Should you force your parents to observe Shabbat in a way that is not their custom? How to achieve a balance—the honor due God and the honor due one's parents—is worthy of thought and discussion.[11]

---

11. If you want to explore this issue further, look at the way the Ten Commandments (Exodus 20:1–14) are laid out. What comes first, honoring God or parents? What are the differences and similarities between these areas? How do these commandments relate to the others in length and content?

9. TEACHER AS PARENT

Bava Metzia 33a–b
Volume II, page 194, line 3–page 202, line 5
Difficulty Factor: 2

This passage, especially the stories on page 197, may be comforting to the beginning Talmud student. There we learn that some very famous sages struggled with the arcane terms they found in the Mishnah and were relieved and grateful when they received answers . . . just like us. Don't worry! Everyone finds something about this sort of study difficult but rewarding. In other words, you're in good company when you're feeling puzzled and in need of a teacher!

In many, many ways, a teacher was considered by the sages to be the equivalent of, and sometimes superior to, a parent. This points to another truth: we have—if we are lucky—many parents in our lives. Our actual parents gave us life, but teachers, rabbis, psychotherapists, and mentors can also parent us as we develop. It is also somewhat comforting as a parent to realize that generally we cannot do it all for our children. We eventually share some of the parenting role with others.

The Mishnah here is straightforward and should be easy to understand. Please remember, the Mishnah is a theoretical document. This outlining of relationships is an *idea* more than a prescription. As parents, that may make the Mishnah's system of priorities easier to take. We have been dealing in this chapter of the Talmud, in part, with the details of the Torah's injunction to help load and unload animals (Exodus 23:5). The Mishnah states that one must unload for one's teacher before unloading for one's father. Note the two little words, *shelimdo ḥokhmah*, "that taught him wisdom" (p. 194, line 7), for the Gemara will end up concentrating on the precise definition of them.

Even though the Mishnah allows us to be more interested in ourselves than in others (again, legislating minimum behavior), the Gemara immediately urges us to go beyond this sort of self-interest, which is ultimately destructive to society and our own humanity. Now the Gemara embarks on a discussion of who exactly qualifies as a teacher. (Although, read the Note on page 196, which will be gratifying to anyone who pays the bills!) The stories that follow, showing how much teachers and learning were valued, are touching. Teachers and mentors affect our lives profoundly, and sharing stories such as those on page 197, about how grateful we are to them, enriches us emotionally for it can inspire us to teach and mentor others just as we ourselves were taught and mentored. For example, there was one sage, Rabbi Meir, who was so devoted to his teacher, Elisha ben Abuya, that even after the latter apostatized, he would spend time with him and learn from him, and he mourned him after his death (*Ḥagigah* 15a–b).

The Background entry on page 197 about the different ways sages learned in the Land of Israel versus in Babylonia is quite important. Many scholarly works have been written about the differences between the Judaism practiced in these two places and the way scholarship was passed on. This is quite similar to the way we contrast Judaism in America and in the State of Israel today. You might want to take time to discuss and outline these differences and keep them in mind as you continue studying Talmud to see how little has changed over the last 1,500 years.[12]

An aside: You will often see strange entries under "Language (Rashi)," as on page 197. Since Rashi lived in France, he would translate into French many terms from the Talmud for his students. This very old form of French, preserved in Rashi's comments, is studied by scholars of the French language who are interested in that tongue's older roots.

Our passage deals, on page 198, with the question of how to cope with the havoc it wreaks on a relationship when the "parent" figure becomes dependent on the "child." And indeed, even the mere mention of this question in a theoretical way harmed the student–teacher/parent–child relationship between Rav Ḥisda and Rav Huna. As you read this passage you may become uncomfortable. What was with these men? Why were they so intense and competitive? Why didn't they act in a more dignified manner, the way we imagine sages should have acted? One of the greatest strengths of the Talmud is that it does not hide the fierce, competitive, idiosyncratic nature of the sages from us. They

---

12. If you want to read more on this subject, *Rabbinic Instruction in Sasanian Babylonia* is a good, if technical, exploration of the subject (see the For Further Reading section).

loved what they were doing and were passionate about it. (By the way, forty years is a way of saying "a generation" and forty days was a decent period of separation.)

The Gemara, after providing these four stories about student–teacher relationships, now returns to a discussion of the Baraita we read on page 196, lines 3–6. It might be helpful to place the viewpoints of the different sages along this continuum:

Most restrictive definition   Least restrictive definition

Place These Opinions on the Continuum

1. Rabbi Meir: teacher = Talmud teacher, not teacher of Scripture or Mishnah
2. Rabbi Yehudah: teacher = one who taught a person most of his knowledge, whether Scripture, Mishnah, or Talmud
3. Rabbi Yose: teacher = someone who taught even one Mishnah

We see that the law, parsed in accordance with Rav Sheshet, follows Rabbi Yose: the widest possible definition of a teacher is used. Anyone who has taught you Torah is your teacher. (Rav Sheshet, by the way, was one of the greatest scholars of his day and was, according to the Talmud, blind. Disabilities need not prevent a person from becoming a great teacher.)

On page 199, the Gemara wonders how Rabbi Yoḥanan could say that the law follows Rabbi Yehudah, that is, only one who taught a person most of his or her knowledge is a teacher, when the Mishnah here seems to imply that a teacher is one who taught wisdom, that is, Talmud specifically, à la Rabbi Meir. In general, Rabbi Yoḥanan follows the anonymous voice of the Mishnah (see p. 297 in the *Reference Guide* for more on this concept). The Gemara answers that wisdom can mean any Jewish knowledge, which was Rabbi Yehudah's view.

> *Feeling frustrated? Don't get this dispute? Don't worry! Just skip it! It's not that important to understand every single item right now. Better to skip something like this and come back to it later than to stick with it and get frustrated. That's a legitimate course of study. Believe me, the Talmud will not run out of interesting things to teach you if you skip some things that are too hard for now.*

Beginning with line 5 on page 199 and through page 200, line 3, we see the sages' ambivalence about what is more important: studying the Bible, Mishnah, or Gemara. Rabbi's ambivalence about the priority of Gemara and Mishnah reflects the sorts of swings we have seen in educational philosophy in our own day. Sometimes we emphasize creativity and then the pendulum swings toward a "back to the basics" attitude. Of course, you need a balanced mix of both and, as you have no doubt concluded yourself, there is no real priority: it is best learned all together. It would be like trying to determine which spoonful of soup is the tastiest: you can't really decide since everything is all mixed together.

Finally, the chapter closes with two somewhat complicated Midrashim that reveal the rather embattled state of mind in which the sages found themselves. From these two expositions, it is clear that there was some tension within the scholarly community and between the scholarly community and the average Jew. This is still true to this day, and we should actually find comfort in the fact that, if previous generations survived this sort of tension, we will probably be able to do so, too.

As you see, from page 200, line 5, through the end of the chapter, we have some statements of Rabbi Yehudah bar Il'ai. This is a common phenomenon. One statement of a teacher is mentioned because it is germane to the topic, and more of that same teacher's sayings are brought into the text as well. Again, this is like footnotes that find their way into the primary text. The teaching on page 201, line 4, is important. When we are experts or role models, especially in Judaism, we must take care to scrupulously practice what we preach. For example, if the rabbi is out eating a ham sandwich in public, then everyone who witnesses the event will think, "Well, if the rabbi eats ham sandwiches, then it must be okay to do so."

The chapter is rounded out with a word of comfort known as a *nehemta*. Again, you may feel repelled by the negativism you see here, on page 202, toward laypersons and even other sages. However, the passage ends by grouping all Jews together in happiness, and idol worshipers are cast as the enemy. Even this may seem unfitting to a modern reader. Think of it in terms of Jews in Nazi Germany saying this about their oppressors and it may make more sense. Remember, idol worshipers were not just theologically repugnant to the sages but could be politically and militarily dominant as well, so such statements are not only theological, but political in nature.

10. BUSINESS ADVICE

Bava Metzia **42a**
Volume II, page 328, line 1–page 330, line 8
Difficulty Factor: 5

> *Okay. Get ready for a passage that is a little tougher than the norm. You're probably going to want to give yourself a good bit of time to study this passage, and you might want to make an outline of it to help see how it's put together. As always, if working on this passage makes you feel too frustrated or discouraged, don't feel bad about skimming it now and coming back to it. Get out of it what you can now and know that you'll be able to return to it after you have studied more Talmud; it will probably go more easily at that time.*

To prepare for reading this passage, do the following:

1. **Read Deuteronomy 14:22–29**, which outlines the tithes.

2. **Refresh your memory** on the subject by reading about it in the Introduction to this volume or looking up these relevant entries in the *Reference Guide*:

Bikkurim: page 167, column 2, 5th entry
Leket: page 209, column 1, 3rd entry
Ma'aser oni: page 221, column 1, 4th entry
Ma'aser rishon: page 221, column 2, last entry
Ma'aser sheni: page 222, column 1, 1st entry
Ma'aserot: page 222, column 1, 2nd entry
Pe'ah: page 243, 1st entry under the letter Pey
Terumah: page 275, column 1, 2nd entry
Terumat ma'aser: page 275, column 2, 3rd entry

3. **Bring in some actual produce** (e.g., one hundred blueberries) and try dividing up and sectioning off the various por-

tions required by Jewish law: *leket, shekhiḥah, bikkurim, terumah, ma'aser rishon, ma'aser sheni, ma'aser oni,* and *pe'ah.* You'll need someone to role-play being a farmer, a beggar, a gleaner, a Levite, and a Kohen (i.e., priest) to be able to allot the food to the proper categories of persons. If you wanted to make an analogy to today, you could say that a person should take his or her income and allot it to Jewish causes, Zionist causes, outright gifts to the poor, and so on. If this system seems complicated to you, you'll be relieved to know that many people apparently had trouble with it in ancient days and were lax in observing these rules.

We have here a classic example of the way the Gemara spiritualizes the physical world of the Mishnah. The Mishnah is involved in concrete realities: how one guards a quantity of money correctly. And how is that? By holding on to it carefully, not even putting it in a sack over his or her shoulder. It is, of course, interesting to note that there were pickpockets and burglars in the days of the Mishnah, as today. It is both encouraging and discouraging to see how little human behavior has changed.

The Gemara now examines the Mishnah's strictures. As often happens, it brings the ruling of a great sage, here Rabbi Yitzḥak, and then brings other teachings by him that are not completely germane to the Mishnah's subject. Then the Gemara continues to comment on the themes brought up in these other teachings: it's like footnotes to footnotes. You could outline this passage in the following way:

1. Mishnah: page 328, lines 1–4
2. Gemara exploring Mishnah: page 328, lines 5–6
3. Rabbi Yitzḥak's teaching about money over one's shoulder: page 328, lines 7–9
4. Three more of Rabbi Yitzḥak's teachings, page 329: (a) lines 1–2, (b) lines 3–6, (c) lines 7–8
5. A different version of Rabbi Yitzḥak's teaching (c): lines 9–10
6. An elaboration of Rabbi Yitzḥak's teaching (c) and the different version of it (# 5): page 330, lines 1–8

You might want to use different colored markers to label each section to make these different sources clearly visible.

As the Gemara explores the nature of blessings, tithings, and measuring, it subtly brings out a point exactly opposite of the Mishnah: it is by giving away material goods, by storing them away and by *not* counting them obsessively, that we obtain blessings for ourselves. As so often happens in the Talmud, both the Mishnah and the Gemara are correct: there are times for counting and holding and there are times for giving up and putting away material wealth. The trick for each of us as persons is knowing when to do which![13]

11. WHAT IS OWNING? ACQUIRING? MONEY?

Bava Metzia 44a (Mishnah 4:1)
Volume III, page 3, line 1–page 6, line 3
Difficulty Factor: 5

Is that the theme from the Twilight Zone *you hear? If it is, I wouldn't be surprised because you really are about to enter another dimension. Imagine you were trying to explain to someone from 1,500 years ago how credit cards work. "Well," you'd say, "you give the cashier this piece of plastic, and she sends a piece of paper with the amount of money you spent and your number to a bank and the bank gives her the money and you pay a bill a month later and . . ." You'd already have been interrupted about six times by questions because the whole thing would be so foreign to your guest. Now reverse the situation. This Mishnah is going to demonstrate how commercial transactions were accomplished in ancient days. Again, if this sort of thing confuses you and you're frustrated by this passage, just tell yourself you'll come back to it.*

One of the most difficult parts of traveling to a foreign country is learning how to manipulate the monetary system and equating it to American dollars. This passage gives us the opportunity to become familiar with the monetary system in use in the sages'

---

13. You might have an investment professional study this passage with you (particularly p. 329, lines 3–6) and compare Rabbi Yitzḥak's business advice with current financial thinking.

day. In preparation for studying this passage you might want to do the following:

1. **Read the article on coins** in the *Reference Guide*, pages 290–292.

2. **Read the Introduction** to Volume III, pages 1–2.

3. **Glance through the Realia entries** in this volume on pages 11, 17, and 19, and the Background entries on pages 58 and 59 before you start studying this Mishnah in order to get an idea of what the passage is talking about.

This is a great passage for examining what an incredible achievement this translation of the Talmud is. The Commentary, which should be read carefully, makes the Mishnah understandable when it would not be otherwise. This is also a nice place to reflect on how much commentary we need to bridge the gap between our time and the sages'. Just compare the size of the Translation and Commentary to the Literal Translation on page 3 and you'll immediately grasp the point.

To understand this Mishnah you might want to do some role-playing of what acquires what using American coins as "pinch hitters" for the coins mentioned in the Mishnah. In addition, you might want to role play the different modes of acquisition outlined in the Concepts entry on page 3. You could look up these entries in the *Reference Guide*:

Hagbahah: page 181, column 1, 1st entry
Halifin: page 192, column 1, 1st entry
Hazakah: page 189, column 2, last entry
Kinyan: page 254, column 1, last entry
Meshikhah: page 224, column 1, 6th entry
Mesirah: page 220, column 1, last entry

Or you can follow the description of it here. Imagine how you would have to describe, step-by-step, our modes of acquisition today, for example, by credit card, by cash, by mortgage, and so on. When would you say that the act of acquisition has irrevocably taken place today? When you give the sales clerk your credit card? When you carry the merchandise away in a bag? When you write the check for the credit-card bill? When you clip the tags off the item? When you use the item you purchased?

These questions also interested the sages. They developed various ways to transfer movable property. (Obviously, real estate required specialized methods of transfer, just as it does today.) Let's briefly look at the ways a person can acquire things in the sages' world. First of all, the idea that "possession is nine-tenths of the law" finds its corollary in the concept of *hazakah*. If a person has possessed an item, or property, for an uninterrupted period of time, he or she is presumed to be in ownership of that property or item. Let's say you bought a truck and found in one compartment a set of jumper cables. You don't know how they got there but you keep them for awhile and then we consider them yours. The simplest way of acquiring things that aren't in your possession is probably *hagbahah*, or lifting up. If you want to take possession of jumper cables, you lift them up and they are yours, even if you have not yet handed over the money for them. However, what if you are buying a couch that you cannot lift up? You can either drag it toward you and then it is yours (this is called *meshikhah*) or the seller can push it toward you, for example, toward your truck, if you bought it at a garage sale (this is called *mesirah*). Now, let's say you want this couch from this garage sale and you don't have any money. However, you have the jumper cables in your truck and the garage sale operator wants them. You agree to exchange the jumper cables for the couch. As soon as the garage saler pulls the jumper cables toward himself, you own the couch even though you haven't touched it. This is called *halifin*. (This can also be accomplished by using a handkerchief symbolically.) All these procedures are different types of *kinyan*, acquisition. Notice, please, that the exchange of money has little to do with determining the exact moment of acquisition. It's possessing, holding, or moving that defines that moment.

This Mishnah uses a specialized example to explore the questions under study: what is money and what is acquisition? A modern-day analogy would be the purchase of a commemorative coin with cash. Both are money but one is the acquired item and one is the money it is bought with.

In the Notes on page 6, you will see that there is a discussion about the words "this is the general principle" and how they do not appear in every manuscript of the Talmud. The Talmud evolved slowly over centuries, in many places, and was copied by hand. Additions and deletions (and errors) occurred in this transmission over time. This does not mean a variant text is less valuable or less authentic. It's just a fact that should be dealt with, especially when the different versions in different manuscripts cause confusion or point to philosophical differences between different schools.[14]

On page 6 we see the strong condemnation the sages bring against a person who does not keep his or her word in a business transaction. It is as bad as the violence practiced by the generation of Noah (see Genesis 6:5–13, not Genesis 5:5–13, as misprinted in the text) and the hubris of those who built the tower of Babel (a not-so-subtle putdown of the ancient Babylonian religion and its huge ziggurats), recounted in Genesis 11:1–9. Of course, a strong moral condemnation in this context connotes an inability to enforce the desired behavior legally. What commercial behaviors today fall into the same category, behaviors that are legal but "toe the line," as it were?

This whole Mishnah raises important issues for us as Americans. The whole role of commerce, acquisition, and owning in our lives is one that needs examination. What does owning property do for us? Is it a behavior we should practice more frequently or less frequently? When is owning helpful? Hurtful?[15]

12. THE COMMERCE OF PERCEPTIONS AND FEELINGS

Bava Metzia 58b
Volume III, page 223, line 2–page 251, line 8
Difficulty Factor: 1

If I were just starting to study Talmud and I wanted to pick the easiest and most relevant passage to work on, this would be the

---

14. There is a whole book, called *Diqduqei Sofrim*, which details these variant texts as well as a computer program with even more information on this topic. Scholars examine these variant texts from the manuscripts of the Talmud to learn more about the sages' world and the process of transmission the Talmud has undergone over the centuries. If you want to see what this is like, consult a local teacher or rabbi.

15. You might want a banker or certified public accountant to explain to you how transactions take place from his or her point of view and how this corresponds, or does not correspond, to the Mishnah's commercial system.

one I would choose. It is all about the importance and reality of
feelings and it is quite easy to understand.

This passage is one of the longest ones we will study and the
one that may be easiest to understand because it talks about human
feelings. While so many other things have changed in the 1,500
years that have elapsed since the sages' day, feelings have not
changed one bit, apparently. Hurt feelings are still painful to those
who experience them and dangerous for those who inflict them.

This passage, from page 223 to page 241, deals with varying
definitions of *ona'ah*, harming someone either monetarily or emotionally. This word comes from the Hebrew root *yud-nun-hey*,
which means to oppress and, interestingly, to be undecided, to
waver, or to discourage. This passage is actually quite easy to
understand and Rabbi Steinsaltz's Commentary provides you
with almost everything you need. Just a few guidelines for its
study are provided here.

On page 227, we find some conflicting traditions about Gehinnom, that is, the Jewish version of Hell. This may surprise many
first-time students of Talmud, who thought that Judaism doesn't
believe in Hell.[16] The Background entry on page 227 hints at our
current practice of saying kaddish for eleven months. Since the
wicked are thought to be judged in Gehinnom for twelve months,
we say kaddish for our parents for eleven months only, lest we
imply that our parents were evil enough to be judged for an entire
twelve-month period.

On page 227, line 6, we learn that there are three crimes so
heinous that those who commit them never rise out of Gehinnom,
unlike the average sinner who spends twelve months in Gehinnom and then rises. A man who commits adultery with a married woman, someone who shames someone else in public, and
someone who calls someone else by a bad name are never allowed
to rise. Of course, the common denominator of these sins is that
they involve shaming someone else.

The Gemara now goes on to examine each of these sins in detail. What follows (p. 228, line 2–p. 229, line 4) is a charming, but
difficult, story about David that involves a good bit of punning

---

16. If you are interested in this topic, you might want to look at the article
entitled "Netherworld" in the *Encyclopaedia Judaica*, volume 12, pp. 996–998.

in Hebrew. If you find this too difficult, just skip it and start up
again on page 229, line 5. If you decide you want to cover it, the
Notes and Background are particularly helpful here, as well as
the Commentary with the Translation. (Especially important is
the Note on page 229, which states that it is sinful to speak ill of
other people, even if what is said is true.)[17]

On page 229, line 5, the discussion continues with the details
of the sin of shaming others in public. Though the story of Tamar
is summarized on page 230, line 2, you might want to read it in
its entirety in Genesis 38. The Commentary here is quite complete
in explaining how this story relates to our topic.

In line 3 on page 230 we once more have a pun in the Hebrew.

> *Again, if this doesn't make sense, just mark it and say, "I'll be com-
> ing back to this later when I know more." When you do this, don't
> feel bad. Nobody understands everything in a Talmud passage on
> the first pass. That's why the Talmud is a classic. You can read
> the same passage repeatedly and get something different out of it
> each time.*

In line 5, page 230, we learn of a teaching by Rav about the
seriousness of hurting one's wife's feelings. It will help us to
understand this statement, and Rav's next statement about wives
(p. 231, line 5) if we know about his own married life, as we learn
in another place in the Talmud:

> Rav was constantly tormented by his wife. If he told her, "Prepare
> me lentils," she would prepare for him small peas; [and if he asked
> for] small peas, she prepared him lentils. When his son Ḥiyya grew
> up he gave her [his father's instructions] in the reverse order. Rav
> said to him [Ḥiyya], "Your mother has improved!" He [Ḥiyya] said
> to him [Rav], "It was I who reversed [your orders] to her." He [Rav]
> said to him, "This is what people say: 'Your own offspring teaches
> you reason'; you, however, must not continue to do so, for it is said,
> 'They have taught their tongue to speak lies; they weary themselves
> to commit iniquity' (Jeremiah 9:4)." (*Yevamot* 63a)

---

17. You might want to glance at the tractates of *Nega'im* and *Ohalot* in the
Mishnah. These are incredibly difficult tractates having to do with ritual purity
and leprosy.

Clearly, Rav had a difficult relationship with his wife. This may be the source of his heartfelt exposition on 1 Kings 21:25 found in lines 5 and 6 of page 231. King Ahab was apparently a decent king until he took the advice of his wife Jezebel. Rav makes this a general rule that a man should not listen to his wife's advice. In line 7 on page 231, we see a different opinion expressed by Rav Pappa that a person should listen to his wife's counsel. Note carefully that Rav and Rav Pappa are not having an argument in person. You might want to look on page 32 of the *Reference Guide* under the column labeled "Babylonia" to see how far apart in time these two sages lived. Rather, these represent two opposing views, possibly based on personal experience, which are likely to be found in every generation. While these two statements are arranged in chronological order, they may also reflect the ideas of an editor who tends to put the statement that is most widely accepted last in a passage. Then the anonymous redactor of the Gemara steps in and tries to elucidate what the true difference between these two points of view in lines 8 and 9 is. There is, in fact, probably no way to resolve these two viewpoints, nor should we try to do so: they accurately reflect the experiences of different groups of people and should be allowed to stand as they are.

On page 232 we have three metaphorical images of the ways that God reacts quickly to hurt feelings: through a gate, through God's direct intervention, and through the drawing aside of a curtain before heaven. In the Translation and Commentary of line 1 on this page, you may be surprised to learn that angels guard the gates of heaven. You might not have thought that Jews believe in angels and, indeed, some sages in the Rabbinic era apparently did not. However, some sages clearly did believe in angels and many lay persons certainly did. God's retinue was thought to resemble a Babylonian monarch's court. There were angels representing the 70 nations of the world and ministering angels who served God as advisors.[18] This points to a solution of a critical problem we face today. Many Jews abandon Judaism and adopt other religions in their search for a mystical relationship with God that may involve a belief in angels. They believe that

---

18. For more on this topic you might want to see the article "Angels and Angelology" in the *Encyclopaedia Judaica*, volume 2, pp. 955–977.

they cannot find such a path to God within Judaism. They are in error. A Jew should search his or her own tradition first before looking for religious answers elsewhere because there is scarcely a path to God that cannot be found in Judaism.

The image of the plumbline here (p. 232, lines 1–2) is a bit difficult. Again, if you can't quite grasp it, just go on and don't feel bad about it. If you'd like to understand it more fully, it will help you to read the whole passage in Amos:

> Thus the Lord God showed me; and behold, He formed locusts in the beginning of the shooting up of the latter growth; and, lo, it was the latter growth after the king's mowings. And if it had come to pass, that when they made an end of eating the grass of the land—so I said, "O Lord God, forgive, I beseech You; how shall Jacob stand? for he is small." The Lord repented concerning this; "It shall not be," says the Lord. Thus the Lord God showed me; and, behold, the Lord God called to contend by fire; and it devoured the great deep and would have eaten up the land. Then said I: "O Lord God, cease, I beseech You; how shall Jacob stand?" for he is small. The Lord repented concerning this; "This also shall not be," says the Lord God. Thus He showed me; and behold, the Lord stood beside a wall made by a plumbline, with a plumbline in His hand. And the Lord said unto me: "Amos, what do you see?" And I said, "A plumbline." Then said the Lord: "Behold, I will set a plumbline in the midst of My people Israel; I will not again pardon them any more; and the high places of Isaac shall be desolate, and the sanctuaries of Israel shall be laid waste; and I will rise against the house of Jeroboam with the sword." (Amos 7:1–9)

It could be that God, dropping the plumbline directly from heaven down to earth, circumvents all the normal intermediaries and that we can pick up the end of the line and talk to God directly as if it were a "telephone" of string with two paper cups. Finally, there are three sins that are thought to come before God immediately and this list is based on *drashot* of certain Biblical verses (p. 233, lines 1–4).

Again, if you can make the connection with the passage, great. If not, come back to it after further study and let this serve as your own personal "plumbline" to measure how much you've learned.

Now we have some very nice sayings about the importance of honoring one's wife and maintaining one's household adequately (p. 233, line 5–p. 234, line 4). These are pretty straightforward and easy to understand with the commentary. You might want to try the following exercise for page 226, line 1–page 234, line 4: highlight in a given color all the lines in this passage that deal directly with relations between a husband and wife. Then highlight in another color all the lines that deal with *ona'ah* that relate a Rabbinic concept to a Biblical verse. You might even want to make a copy of the pages, cut out the passages, rearrange them in a way that makes more sense to you, and then put them back together. This is a very fun way of learning about a scholarly method of studying the Talmud called source criticism. It could be that the sages had a collection of teachings about husband–wife relationships and about *ona'ah* and that they were spliced together here in a way that may be a little bit hard for us to follow. This way of studying Talmud, that is, examining how it is put together, is very much like working on a jigsaw or crossword puzzle. Seeing how the Talmud was put together is delightful and just another path into this document, which may occasionally seem difficult to understand.

What follows now (p. 234, line 5–p. 239, line 9) is a long and extremely important and interesting story about hurt feelings. It is all fairly self-explanatory except for the incident that causes all the trouble. To understand this fight about the oven of Akhnai (a picture is found on p. 235) we need to know that for an object to be susceptible to ritual impurity, it must fit into the category of a whole object, in this case, a whole oven. Likewise, for an object to be unsusceptible to ritual purity, it cannot fit into the category of a whole object. For example, if we were having this fight today, you would find a dead animal, let's say a small lizard, of the sort that are frequently found in the South, in your oven. It had simply crawled in there and died without your seeing it. But this would make your oven ritually impure since this animal had died in it. So the question is, if you disassemble your oven so that it no longer fits our cultural category of "working oven," can you reassemble the parts and use the oven again? Rabbi Eliezer allows us to use this convenient and cost-efficient remedy to our problem. All the rest of the sages do not allow us to do so. They say the oven is off limits forever and that anything prepared in this oven is ritually impure. Because Rabbi Eliezer makes a public argument over this issue and refuses to go along with the majority, he is excommunicated and the hurt feelings that result cause great destruction.[19] In all of this passage, which you can understand on many levels of your own making, the message is borne home: hurt feelings are real, to people and to God.

How are we to understand this story? We can certainly understand it on the level of metaphor. The tree and water are both symbols of Torah, and Rabbi Eliezer is uprooting and reversing the Torah, as it were. Perhaps the argument between Rabbi Eliezer and the sages was so fierce that it seemed to threaten the very existence of the Academy, almost making its walls fall in, as it were. The destruction of one-third of the olive, wheat, and barley crops (p. 238, line 7) could be a retaliatory action against the sages by Rabbi Eliezer's followers. Since the sages symbolically burned what Rabbi Eliezer called pure, perhaps Rabbi Eliezer's supporters burned crops that the sages called pure.

While we can understand the story on the level of metaphor, we should also allow it to speak to us on the level of legend or myth. This is a dramatic tale, told with dramatic flair. In short, it has elements of truth, of morality, and of entertainment all together at the same time. We can get the most out of this story, and others like it, when we understand it on many levels rather than trying to view it in just one way. The Talmud speaks in 70 tongues and it is a pleasure to listen to as many of them as possible.

We can use this "multilayered" method in understanding Rabban Gamliel's perilous trip (p. 238, line 9–p. 239, line 1). On the one hand, we can see the swelling sea as a metaphor: the excommunication of Rabbi Eliezer threatened to drown Rabban Gamliel's leadership. On the other hand, we can understand the story in a straightforward way. God can speak to us through natural phenomena. God is constantly communicating with us in diverse ways. What varies is our ability and willingness to listen to the messages.

---

19. Rabbi Steinsaltz has written a charming account of this passage, which might help you better understand it: "The Downfall of Rabbi Eliezer" in *The Strife of the Spirit*, pp. 136–149 (see the For Further Reading section).

The story with Rabbi Eliezer's wife, Imma Shalom, on page 239, lines 2–8, shows how a woman could be learned and recite teachings of the sages authoritatively. We note, too, that Imma Shalom is one of the few people who seems to be able to control Rabbi Eliezer, although she must maintain extraordinary vigilance to do so. Again, we could understand this story on a metaphorical level. Rabbi Eliezer, though excommunicated, would have had many supporters remaining in the Academy, and they might eventually have overcome Rabban Gamliel, "killing," as it were, his leadership of the Academy.

On page 240, line 1–page 241, line 5, we learn how serious an offense it is to hurt the feelings of someone who has converted to Judaism. This is particularly important for us today since so often, years after a conversion and faithful observance of Judaism, Jews will still say, "Oh, she used to be a *shiksah*." This is absolutely forbidden. Once a person has converted to Judaism, he or she is considered to be like a newborn child. Nothing he or she did before the conversion is held to be relevant. The expositions in these lines are punning on the fact that the word *ger* can mean either stranger or convert.

How are we to understand Rabbi Eliezer's statement on page 241, line 3, that a convert's inclination is bad? Today we can occasionally, sadly, see an example of this phenomenon when a person has converted to Judaism, married a Jew, and then divorced. Sometimes, in the bitterness of the divorce, the person will renounce his or her conversion to Judaism. This is an example of a way in which "mistreating them may cause them to return to their former ways."

The teaching on page 241, lines 5–6, about being careful with your words seems funny at first. However, the sages are simply suggesting that we be tactful and thoughtful. To avoid hurting people's feelings, we should be able to put ourselves in others' shoes and intuit what might offend them.

On page 241 we begin a passage with two Mishnahs and the commentary on them involving *ona'ah* of deception. These passages are fairly self-explanatory. In fact, this might be material that you want to read with the Literal Translation only, referring to the Translation and Commentary only when necessary. These passages are also interesting in terms of the history of the period and the practices with regard to wine and food that are recorded here. It is fascinating that human commerce has changed so little in 1,500 years. Merchants are constantly struggling for an edge, and lawsuits over price-cutting tactics are carried out to this day.

You will notice on page 244, lines 1–2, that the Gemara remarks on one phrase in the Mishnah, "In truth they said" (p. 242, line 2). This is because the Mishnah was designed to be memorized and thus is very rhythmic, logical, and simple in its formulations. There are rarely any superfluous words in the Mishnah, so a phrase such as "In truth they said," which is not strictly necessary, stands out and almost begs to be remarked upon.

Another tendency seen in this passage is characteristic of the Talmud: the respect for local custom (e.g., p. 243, line 1). The sages wanted to achieve the fine balance between a unified practice for the Jewish people and respect for local custom. There never has been such a thing as "homogenized" Judaism. In fact, one of Judaism's great strengths is its flexibility and ability to adapt to local conditions. Here, the sages affirm this principle—*minhag hamakom*, [respect for] the custom of a place—as a positive trait.

An interesting incident is related in the passage on page 246, line 5–page 247, line 2. In what is apparently a real case, Rava disregards the ruling of the Mishnah and returns diluted wine to a wine merchant. As we have noted before, the Mishnah is a theoretical document and did not always correspond to real life. Here, an eminent sage acted with great latitude in relation to the Mishnah's rulings.

Our next Mishnah (page 247, line 6–page 248, line 5) concerns practices designed to make merchandise appear better than it is, thus allowing a merchant to charge more for it. It is interesting that, as we learn on page 250, lines 3–5, several sages permitted decorations on merchandise. It would seem that merchants took the rulings of the Mishnah to heart and consulted sages when they wished to improve the appearance of their merchandise. Note how all these sages were quite lenient in allowing the decoration of merchandise. Were all sages lenient in this regard? Or did the editor of the Gemara simply choose to record lenient rulings? We cannot know, but it would appear that sages were consulted to some extent on matters of commerce.

Our whole passage ends with the story on page 251. This is a standard literary device: rounding out a composition with a story that ends with a Biblical verse promising reward and comfort for righteous behavior. It is a fitting summation for a long passage concerned with righteousness in business and in relationships.

This is the end of this chapter. When people finish an entire tractate of the Talmud, they sometimes have a party. You might have such a party after you finish this passage, especially if it is the first one you have ever studied. This is an achievement: you opened the book and learned. You're part of the chain of tradition now!

13. EVERYTHING IS CONNECTED: A MYSTICAL MIDRASH

Bava Metzia 61b
Volume IV, page 19, line 3–page 24, line 9
Difficulty Factor: 4

This passage is fun in that, once you understand the dishonest business practices outlined here, you'll have no problem relating them to similar scams you yourself may have experienced. This passage is particularly encouraging to consumers because it suggests that those who employ shady business practices will eventually pay a price for it . . . a very nice thought indeed!

It is a commonplace in mystical teaching that everything is connected and nothing is hidden from God. Our innermost thoughts and supposedly secret deeds all play a role in the repair or ruination of the world. The Midrash that we will read in this passage teaches that the Exodus from Egypt, not charging interest, honesty in business practices, and refraining from eating creeping things are all related to each other.

To understand this passage, it will help you to do the following:

1. Look over Leviticus 19:1–36. This is the Holiness Code, which is basically a restatement of the Ten Commandments.

2. Read the following entry in the *Reference Guide*:

Kal vaḥomer: page 153, column 2, 3rd entry

You might want to stop after the first paragraph of this entry; the second paragraph gets a bit technical. Basically, *kal vaḥomer* means "all the more so." For example, if it is good to strike out one batter, *kal vaḥomer*, all the more so is it good to pitch a no-hitter.

3. You will also want to read the Introduction to this chapter on pages 1–2 of this volume.

First, the passage explores the prohibition against stealing (p. 19, line 3–p. 21, line 6) and how stringent it is. Any business practice that is in the least unfair is considered stealing. If all these measurements seem confusing, you might want to consult the *Reference Guide* again about Weights and Measures.[20]

We then begin another, extended Midrash on page 22, line 1, that runs through the end of page 24. The Midrash here relates different laws to each other because at their source, in the Torah, they are all connected to the phrase, "I am the Lord your God, who brought you out of the Land of Egypt." (On the simple level, when a law is stated and is related to a reminder that God brought us out of Egypt, it is to remind us why we owe God allegiance and obedience. It is something like a mother or father saying to a child, "I changed all your diapers so you should listen to me now.") The sages want to know what these verses (Leviticus 25:35–38, Numbers 15:38–41, Leviticus 11:43–45) have in common, and they deduce that they all have to do with dishonesty. Since this is not evident on the face of these verses, the sages now explain and we get a glimpse of some of the shady business practices of ancient days that do not differ too greatly from our own. Apparently, Jews would use inaccurate weights; involve themselves in business deals with interest, which were right on the edge of the allowable; shortchange other Jews in preparing the tassels on prayer shawls; and mix kosher and *treif* fish entrails in

---

20. You might also want to look at Aryeh Carmell's entries on these terms in *Aids to Talmud Study* (New York: Feldheim, 1980), pp. 74–80, since he gives modern equivalents there that might make this material easier to understand.

order to increase profits. The prohibition against making liquids foam (p. 21, line 3) may remind you of the current-day practice of filling a cup with ice so that you really only receive two sips of a soft drink. This, under Jewish law, would be prohibited. Finally (p. 24, lines 4–8), the sages comment on the slightly different word used in the Torah in Leviticus 11:45, which states that God brings us up (*hama'aleh*) rather than simply bringing us out (*hamotzi*). Apparently eating creeping things was deemed especially loathsome by the sages.

This Midrash assures us that justice will eventually be done and that shady business practices will be punished. These are but a few examples of a great religious truth: there is no such thing as getting away with something. The misdeed may be hidden, but then the punishment may be hidden. According to this Midrash, there is justice in the world.

14. NO INSIDER TRADING AND OTHER RULES OF FAIRNESS IN FINANCES

Bava Metzia 75a–75b
Volume IV, page 262, line 1–page 270, line 4
Difficulty Factor: 2

The sort of honesty and integrity in personal and business relationships required by the Talmud here is truly refreshing. Today, if someone is merely honest, instead of scrupulously so, it seems like a great feat. This passage challenges us to go above and beyond and introduce true righteousness into our business relationships. It's a great standard to try to live up to!

We begin this passage with the Mishnah that, in its beautiful and idealistic way, demands absolute equality in all human affairs involving any monetary value. (In fact, the Mishnah is literarily beautiful, too. Try comparing the Literal Translation on p. 262 with the Translation and Commentary, or even the Hebrew, to see how rhythmic and poetic the Mishnah is here.) On page 263, lines 4–7, we learn how far the sages go in keeping relationships honest. Flattery, bribery, even overly florid expressions of gratitude and respect are forbidden. We should be clear, however, that this concerns loans, not regular business practices. We learn, for example, in Volume III, page 248, line 6–page 249, line 1 (60a) that a storekeeper can distribute nuts to attract children to his store.

Furthermore, we learn on page 264, lines 1–3, that we are not allowed to enrich someone who lends us money through information; in other words, there should be no insider trading. We also learn that anyone involved with a loan on interest transgresses Jewish law. This is a concept we might resist, but it is quite important. We might want to limit the number of people who can be found guilty (as the sages did, for example, in capital-punishment cases). But here, the sages blame everyone involved because they could have stopped the transaction or at least refused to participate. The so-called innocent bystander is not allowed to exist in such situations. One either participated or refused to participate.

Why is the prohibition against interest so strong? Because in an agricultural society, it was considered immoral to ask for interest. Rather, one was to make a gift, or at most lend, what a neighbor needed rather than attempting to make money out of a fellow person's need. Later, in a more mercantile society, charging interest came to be seen as a legitimate compensation for risk. This is a prime example of Judaism responding flexibly to changing conditions.

In commenting on this Mishnah, the Gemara (p. 265, lines 5–9) hints at how destructive money can be in human relationships and how careful we must be not to let this happen. On page 266, lines 2–6, Abaye analyzes who exactly in the loan scenario is violating which Torah verses.

The passage continues with further details of the ways we must be careful to preserve human relationships in their proper balance when money is involved. Any practice that might lead, even inadvertently, to an impropriety is condemned in the story involving Rav Ashi and Ravina (p. 268, line 6–p. 269, line 8).

The chapter closes with a teaching (p. 269, line 9–p. 270, line 5) that many modern readers may find insulting. The Baraita is brought because it ties in with the theme of this passage: the negative impact of loans on interest. This is a prime example of a passage about which we might become angry. However, after the first flush of anger we should realize that rage won't help us understand the passage. Is it sexist? Sure. Does it have something valuable to teach? Likewise. The three persons described in this Baraita are ones who have not followed sensible rules of human conduct and therefore have no right to complain to Heaven that things aren't going the way they'd like. The sexist statement could apply equally as well to women as to men. No one's spouse should rule over him or her. Rather, as we have learned elsewhere (e.g., Volume III, p. 230, line 5), husbands and wives should respect each other and consult with each other. The very last page of our chapter, page 270, explores the meaning of placing a master over oneself. In essence, the Gemara suggests that we must take responsibility for our lives and insure our independence, at the same time trying not to be too shrewd. Not bad business advice at all.[21]

15. SUFFERING AND SAGES

Bava Metzia 83a–87a
Volume V, page 111, line 1–page 167, line 11
Difficulty Factor: 2

This is one of the longest passages we will study and one of the ones with the most "plot." If you are interested in stories of the sages and their spiritual adventures, this one and the story of Rabbi Eliezer's downfall (No. 12) are the places to start. Likewise, if you ever wondered where Jewish sympathy for laborers comes from, look no further. The Mishnah that begins this whole passage shows that, ideally, Jews have treated their laborers as persons rather than as revenue-producing machines for centuries.

We learn that part of employing people is feeding them. Not only must we feed our workers, but we have to provide them with

---

21. If you're interested in what became of the laws of interest and other Talmudic regulations in the Middle Ages, see Jacob Katz's *Exclusiveness and Tolerance* (see the For Further Reading section).

dessert. (If you ever wondered how old the Jewish emphasis on eating is, you're certainly justified in saying two millennia!) Then, a general rule is stated on page 111, line 7: everything goes according to local custom. This is one of Judaism's strengths: it adapts to its local environment and allows for flexibility and individuality of communities. The story about the workers (pp. 111–112) seems to indicate that the Jewish workers of Rabbi Yohanan ben Matya's experience could be insatiable in their demands for food.

An extremely important principle, applied in many other places besides this one, is that everything follows local custom. One of Judaism's strengths is that it adapts to the local environment, not only in terms of business practice, but in religious practice, too. Thus, the traditions of Jews in Sephardic countries (e.g., Morocco) differ greatly from those in Ashkenazic countries (e.g., Russia). This is a signal strength of Jewish culture and can be seen even within the United States. For example, Judaism is practiced somewhat differently in the South than in the Northeast.

We learn in the Gemara (p. 113) that part of the travel time to and from work is considered to be part of the job the employer is paying for. Labor was often difficult and draining in those days, and the person who did not have to do a job was considered lucky. Today, it is the person who *has* work who is envied. However, much of the work we do now does not depend on physical strength, as was so often the case in antiquity.

From page 114, line 6, through page 115, line 6, there is an extended Midrash on Psalm 104:20 relating this verse to labor practices of the day. It is worth reading this section of Psalm 104 to see the context of the Midrash:

> Who appoints the moon for seasons; the sun knows his going down. You make darkness, and it is night, wherein all the beasts of the forest do creep forth. The young lions roar after their prey and seek their food from God. The sun rises; they slink away and couch in their dens. Man goes forth unto his work and to his labor until the evening. (Psalm 104:19–23)

Apparently, it was not the custom to go out after nightfall. Night was a time of danger and vulnerability. Even to this day, walking through the Old City in Jerusalem at night is like walking through a tomb. The streets are almost completely deserted.

Then the Gemara brings what will turn out to be an extremely long passage about Rabbi Elazar the son of Rabbi Shimon. As we shall see, Rabbi Elazar's life is marked by the bizarre in many ways: his physical appearance, his sexual prowess, and his ability to bear suffering. Even as a child, he was different, as the following story shows:

> He [Rabbi Shimon] and his son went and hid themselves in the House of Study, [and] his wife brought them bread and a jug of water and they dined. When the decree [against Torah study] became more severe he said to his son, "Women are of unstable temperament: she may be put to the torture and expose us." So they went and hid in a cave. A miracle occurred and a carob tree and a water well were created for them. They would strip their garments and sit up to their necks in sand. The whole day they studied; when it was time for prayers they robed, covered themselves, prayed, and then put off their garments again, so that they should not wear out. Thus they dwelt twelve years in the cave. Then Elijah came and stood at the entrance to the cave and said, "Who will inform the son of Yoḥai that the emperor is dead and his decree annulled?" So they emerged. Seeing a man plowing and sowing, they said, "They forsake life eternal [Torah study] and engage in life temporal [farming]!" Whatever they cast their eyes upon was immediately burnt up. Thereupon a *Bat Kol* (a Heavenly Voice) came forth and said to them, "Have you emerged to destroy My world? Return to your cave!" So they returned and dwelt there twelve months, saying, "The punishment of the wicked in Gehenna is [limited to] twelve months." A *Bat Kol* then came forth and said, "Go forth from your cave!" Thus they issued: Wherever Rabbi Elazar wounded, Rabbi Shimon healed. Said he to him, "My son! You and I are sufficient for the world [our Torah study suffices for the world and everyone else can farm]." (*Shabbat* 33b)

It seems that Rabbi Elazar's whole life, from childhood on, is marked by conflict and cooperation with the foreign authorities of the day and his extreme reaction to that relationship in his life. This is, perhaps, where Rabbi Elazar's story touches our own lives most deeply. How do we relate to the secular world? Does it make us live in a cave, that is, bury our true selves? Does it make us cut parts of ourselves out? Does it induce guilt? Sin? What role should the secular world play in our lives?

From page 119, line 9 through page 125, line 8, we have what students of mine have called a long "locker-room" passage. Everything from page 119, line 1, to page 125, line 8, is a big insert into the main Rabbi Elazar story. You could skip all that material without missing a beat. However, I wouldn't suggest it, for these are fascinating stories about the sages and their sexuality. On page 119, lines 9–18, we learn about Rabbi Elazar's obesity. Apparently, size issues for men existed then as they do today. (One [male] student, on studying this passage [p. 120, lines 4–8] and the Notes on it at the bottom of the page, commented, "Sex, lies and Talmud.") This passage, and the ones that follow, through page 122, line 6, portray the sages as extremely potent sexually yet supremely able to control their sexual energy. Indeed, being a successful sage was likened to being a father, as we saw in another passage in this tractate (No. 9: Teacher as Parent). These sages' physical aspects matched their inner natures. This is an important concept and one that is borne out in our own lives. When we are sick in spirit we often become sick in body. Likewise, a healthy mental and spiritual outlook can aid us in healing our bodies and becoming more physically fit.

This relationship between emotional truths and physical consequences is reflected in the story about Rabbi Yohanan and Reish Lakish in which Rabbi Yohanan's anger causes Reish Lakish to die. This story (p. 123, line 1–p. 125, line 8) shows how a person's fierce anger can destroy those close to him and, eventually, himself. This, too, is confirmed by modern medicine. Type "A" personalities, who are quick to anger, are more likely to suffer physically from their temperament.

The Gemara (p. 125, line 9) then returns to the story of Rabbi Elazar, and we learn of how he brought sufferings upon himself and how his wife became fed up with this behavior. After she leaves, Rabbi Elazar recovers and goes to the House of Study, from which he had been absent for some time.

The matter of the sixty bloodstained garments on page 126, line 19, might need some explanation. Think of it in terms of bringing a sample to a doctor's office for diagnosis and it may become more accessible. Also, prepare yourself to feel some anger at the sages' sexism on page 127, lines 2–5. The sages assumed that people felt boys were more desirable as children than girls. Just remember our suggestion in the Introduction: allow yourself your anger but then get over it for there is still much beautiful material to be discovered in this passage.

On pages 128 and 129 we learn that Rabbi Elazar continued to function in some ways as a living person after his death. First of all, on page 128, lines 4–6, we see an illustration of the following Jewish principle: listening to slander is a greater sin than saying it. After all, if no one would listen, then no one would gossip. As punishment for this sin, Rabbi Elazar has a worm in his ear.

Even after his death, Rabbi Elazar could still issue Halakhic pronouncements, and his body did not decompose. As Rabbi Steinsaltz notes (Background, p. 128), our relationships with people do not end simply because they are deceased. If you want to think of this on a more rational level, you could understand it as people studying Rabbi Elazar's teachings after he died and judging according to his philosophy. On page 129, lines 4–7, we see something that may strike many Jews as quite strange: the townspeople did not suffer because Rabbi Elazar's body was resident in their town. This is known as vicarious atonement, that is, that someone else can take on our sufferings and prevent our pain. Most Jews would associate this notion only with Christianity. However, as we see here and in other places in this passage (p. 134, lines 8–11), this is a Jewish concept as well, although it does not hold such a prominent place in our philosophy.

There may be yet another layer of meaning to the gargantuan, male–female body of Rabbi Elazar. He seems somewhat similar to the very first human being, Adam. This Adam was believed by the sages to be a hermaphrodite, that is, possessing sexual characteristics of both genders. In addition, this Adam was enormous. Before Adam sinned in the Garden of Eden, he was of massive height and extended from one end of the world to the other (*Genesis Rabbah* 19:9 and 21:3), and after the sin, his height was diminished until he reached only 100 cubits, or about 210 feet in height (*Genesis Rabbah* 12:6). (There are alternative versions of this teaching that claim that his height was as high as 900 cubits!) Rabbi Elazar shares many of this mystical, primordial Adam characteristics. He was (spiritually) "born" in earth (the cave), as was Adam. His body is huge, as Adam's was, and is reduced in size (cutting out the basketsful of fat) after his sin. He has male and female characteristics, as the first Adam was said to have had (*Leviticus Rabbah* 14:1). He sins and suffers as Adam did.

There is obviously a great deal going on here that could use serious, scholarly analysis. Could it be that Rabbi Elazar's story has been shaped by the historical forces of its time and by ancient literary paradigms? Could it be that the symbols in this story hearken back to primordial humanity's eternal dilemmas: its original form that was little less than the angels; its androgyny; its sin, subsequent suffering, and atonement; its death that is a doorway to eternal life? It appears that Rabbi Elazar's story may have been shaped to echo these ancient themes. Certainly, the Jewish people was re-creating itself *ex nihilo*, as it were, in this era of history. Perhaps Rabbi Elazar's character is shaped here to make him the new "Adam" of the Jewish people in a new (and hostile) world.[22]

Now we begin a long passage about Rabbi Yehudah HaNasi that will also involve a bit more material about Rabbi Elazar. We learn (pp. 130–131) of the fierce competition between Rabbi Elazar and Rabbi Yehudah. We may find it disappointing that such great sages would allow their egos to be involved in disputes over their studies. However, it is one of the paradoxes of spiritual development that one must have a well-developed ego in order to let go of it appropriately later. This point exactly is made by the Gemara on pages 132–133. The three examples of humble people are those who had a claim to high station and who gave it up because they recognized that someone could better serve in the elevated position.

Now, we learn more details about Rabbi Yehudah HaNasi's sufferings. We see that there is some difference of opinion about them. You can ask anyone who has suffered from kidney stones about how painful they are (p. 132, lines 11–13). Some of Rabbi's sufferings may have been brought on by love, that is, he wanted them to occur, while others just happened to him without his accepting them and beckoning them to himself. These sufferings protect those around him, just as Rabbi Elazar's did.

On page 135 we learn that Rabbi Elazar's son was quite beautiful but had not dedicated himself to Torah study, as his father had. Indeed, he'd become something of a dissolute youth. Rabbi

---

22. If you are interested in how the Gemara is put together, please note that you could jump from page 130, line 8, to page 132, line 10, without missing a beat. Try reading it this way and then as it stands now to understand how much material was interpolated into the passage.

Yehudah, perhaps tempered by his years of suffering, forgets his old rivalry with Rabbi Elazar and acts to bring the boy back into the mainstream. What does he do? He takes him out of the environment in which he is sinning, arranges for him to be shown the extent of Rabbi Yehudah's expectations for him, that is, he is ordained as a rabbi even though he has not yet earned it and puts him in a mentor–student relationship with a relative to watch over him and teach him. These efforts work and Rabbi Elazar's son becomes a great sage. Perhaps Rabbi Yehudah's steps could serve as a guideline for helping troubled youths today. Rabbi Yose's story is brought to a close on page 136 by showing that he was not his father's equal, nor his grandfather's, not because he was ignorant of the Torah but because he did not suffer as his father and his grandfather had.

We then have another story about Rabbi Yehudah HaNasi transforming the wayward grandson of a sage (p. 136, line 13–p. 137, line 6). The Gemara then tells us why Rabbi Yehudah takes such pains to save these children: these acts bring him an eternal reward. On page 138 we learn that if Torah learning can be kept strong in a family for three generations, God will ensure that the Torah will never be forgotten by the descendants of this family. Today, sadly, many families are completely ignorant of the Torah and seem to be cut off from Judaism. It would seem that the Gemara is showing us how to behave and what measures to take in order to ensure that future generations will not be lost to the Jewish people. Part of that course of action is the active involvement of grandparents. Children must rebel against their parents. But if children can see another Jewish role model in their grandparents, then they are more likely to be able to find their own attachment to Judaism. Such efforts take great energy and active intervention, but that is what the task demands.

The theme of our passage, suffering and its role in redemption, is amplified in the stories about Rav Yosef and Rabbi Zera fasting (p. 128, line 13–p. 140, line 3). We may resist the notion that physical suffering can bring spiritual enlightenment. We might rationalize this as the concept that we all know of from exercising or dieting: you endure pain in order to gain some greater goal.

On page 141 the issue of ego in Torah study reemerges, and here Rabbi Steinsaltz's Background entries are quite important. Many people know of the concept of the *lamed-vavniks*, the thirty-six secret, righteous people who keep the world going. It's not that their identity is hidden or that they perform their acts of goodness in secret. It's that people don't see their goodness and that the righteous persons are comfortable with the level of goodness they attain and do not attribute it to any righteousness of their own, but rather to the simple confluence of inherited nature, time, and opportunity. They take no pride in their goodness, just as no one would take pride in being right-handed: it's just one of your characteristics.

This passage does bring out an important issue that cannot be denied: the influence of breeding and heredity on one's nature and destiny. Is it possible to rise above one's heredity in Torah learning? Does heredity help in this regard? What is the importance of family position and inherited tendencies in Jewish life? As always, the Gemara takes a balanced approach: heredity is important but those without ancestral merit can achieve greatness, too. (For example, Rabbi Akiva came from a most humble background but was able to rise to the heights of Jewish leadership.)

From the bottom of page 141 to page 143, line 11, we begin another passage involving Reish Lakish and his relationship to Rabbi Ḥiyya. Here, another great truth is brought out: Talmudic scholarship is not the greatest good the sages knew. Once one achieved great knowledge of the Talmud, one then had to go out and disseminate that knowledge further. To merely stay in the ivory tower was of no great merit. Perhaps we should take Rabbi Ḥiyya's model to heart for our own day and make children experts in one small area of Jewish studies and then make them teachers. This would quickly give them a sense of mastery and high self-esteem among their peers.

Now we have another story about Rabbi Ḥiyya (p. 143, line 12–p. 145, line 1). The sages envisioned the World to Come as an Academy much like the House of Study on earth. Just as the Academy in Israel was arranged in rows, the sages seated in order of greatest learning to least learning, so the sages of every generation would be seated after death in the Academy. In fact, when we study Talmud, we are achieving this vision of immortality for the sages. Have you had the feeling yet that you are sitting with the greatest minds of many centuries? The more you study, the more you'll get to know the sages and the more they will seem to be sitting with you as you learn. (One student suggested that the unnamed rabbi's "charred eyes" (p. 145, line 1) could be the result of pulling "all-nighters" spent studying Rabbi Ḥiyya's Baraitot.)

There is one more story about Rabbi Ḥiyya's spiritual powers (p. 145, line 2–p. 146, line 6). His prayers were so effective that they could not be denied by God. The prayer under discussion on page 145, lines 17–20, is the second prayer in the Amidah in which we pray for the resurrection of the dead. This task will be accomplished by the Messiah, and Rabbi Ḥiyya would therefore have forced the Messiah's arrival prematurely through this prayer.

It may be interesting for us to contemplate what a free agent Elijah seems to be vis-à-vis God. Is there any historical basis for this passage? Or is this simply a folktale about a great and pious rabbi? There is obviously no way of knowing the answer to these questions and we must therefore be most skeptical. However, can you think of a time when the forces of nature, a moment of prayer, and the force of a personality came together in a remarkable way, for example, at a wedding, funeral, birth, or bat mitzvah? Sometimes forces larger than our lives seem to come together in the way that this story relates.

We now return (p. 146, line 7) to the tales of Rabbi Yehudah HaNasi's sufferings. Shmuel was his physician, and elsewhere in the Talmud we learn a great deal about the medicine of this era from his teachings.

On page 147, lines 5–7, we learn about the end of the Mishnaic era and of the closing of the Talmud. Naturally, scholars have debated about the meaning and veracity of these words extensively. Indeed, scholars vary widely in their opinions as to when the Gemara was finished. Some state that it was as late as 800 while others opine that it was as early as 425 C.E. What we have here is the Talmud's vision of its own history. As we have seen from the stories in this long passage, the Talmud is not a history book as we are accustomed to thinking of history. Rather, it is a combination of law, history, folktales and medicine, morality stories, and the like. History *qua* history is not a terribly important category for the sages.

We now have another miraculous story of a great sage's death (p. 148, line 1–p. 152, line 6). Rabbah bar Naḥmani was a great and popular teacher who became unpopular with the secular authorities. Like other great sages, he controlled the forces of nature through his prayer, which, in turn, was made extremely efficacious on account of his great learning. How do we understand the idea that while one is deeply engaged in Torah study, the Angel of Death cannot come near (p. 150, line 9)? When we are truly immersed in Torah study, we become linked with the Eternal and in this way overcome death. You might be surprised that there is an argument between God and the sages in heaven (p. 150, lines 2–6). As we learn in many passages, objective "correctness" is not the point in Judaism. Rather, it is engaging in the dialectic of learning and developing relationships in the process that is the goal.

Since Rabbah's death was a somewhat violent one—he, a famous scholar, was pursued and left for dead in a field—we can well imagine that it took seven days for people to adequately mourn him (p. 151, line 16). Did notes really fall from heaven (p. 151, lines 14–16)? We can think of it as people's feeling so strongly about mourning Rabbah adequately that it felt as if a direct message was received from God. What about the story of the strong wind and the Arab (p. 151, line 17–p. 152, line 6)? Just as we, and sages, have strong emotions, so too in Judaism is God often experienced as having strong emotions. This non-Jew is able to speak directly and respectfully to God. He asks God to show mercy and restraint while mourning and God complies.

Our long collection of tales about the sages now concludes with another tale about an obese sage, although the more obvious connection is God's relationship with a sage and the wind as an instrument of that relationship. What an uplifting way to end this entire section: a sage goes to find physical relief on a hilltop and finds both physical and spiritual refreshment as a consequence. Thus, the whole section ends on an "up" note, indeed.

We now return to our Mishnah (p. 152, line 14). On page 153, line 4, the Gemara emends the Mishnah. This should not surprise us. The Mishnah was taught orally, and different versions of the same teaching surely existed and mistakes in transmission likewise occurred. The Gemara's addition makes the Mishnah much more intelligible. It is something like workers knowing there will always be coffee and donuts. If the employer says, "I'll bring breakfast," the workers may well expect something far above the normal fare (p. 153, lines 4–11).

On page 153, line 12, the Gemara introduces the figure of Abraham in contrast to King Solomon. Abraham is the archetype of hospitality in the Jewish tradition because of the gracious way he treated three strangers (Genesis 18:1–10), who were actually God's angels. This begins a very easily understood Midrash on Abraham's story, which extends through page 165, line 16.

The quantities of food described in Solomon's house (p. 153, lines 2–4) should be taken as a sort of Rabbinic "tall tale" (although living in Texas, and knowing how big a barbecue can become, I find these descriptions plausible). On page 155, lines 4–14, you may be surprised to find that we have quickly leaped from the Midrashic examination of the Torah to an ancient version of the Galloping Gourmet. The inclusion of this material is not as funny as you might think at first glance. To the sages, every facet of life is grist for their mill of holiness. For example, there is a bit of Miss Manners in this passage, as well, on page 161, line 1. This is not meant as a snobbish statement about whose invitations you should accept. Rather, it is similar to when, upon receiving an invitation, you politely (and ritually) say, "I don't want to put you to any bother." The host then answers that it will be no bother at all. However, such a statement would be ludicrous when addressed to, for example, the Rockefellers. For persons of such wealth, company would not be an imposition.

On page 162, line 3, we learn that one sage felt that women might not have been as hospitable as men. Was this simply his individual view? Or were women then, as women now, put out when their husbands suddenly announced that they were bringing home extra company for dinner? Or is this simply sexism? Here is a place where it is good not to become fixated on or angry at one statement but attempt to understand it, react to it, and move on.

On page 163, lines 7–9, we learn about a word in Genesis 18:9 that has dots over it.[23] Many theories have been advanced regarding these dots. They may point to special meanings in these words, as suggested by Rabbi Steinsaltz. Others suggest that they were meant to signify erasures.

On page 165 under the Background entry "Until Abraham there was no old age," and the passage there (p. 165, line 12–p. 166,

---

23. It is worthwhile to actually look this up in a Torah scroll if you have a chance.

line 9), you will find some somewhat playful interpretations of
Torah. The enjoyment we get out of puns, crossword puzzles,
wordsearch games, and so forth, previous generations found in
Torah. It is too bad that we have lost the sense of fun in studying
Torah. Torah is serious, yes, but there is no human condition that
is not reflected in it; fun, games, and humor are a large and precious part of human experience and, therefore, of Torah.

From page 165, line 17, through page 166, line 7, we finish this
section with an examination of illness, especially the illness of
Elisha. Elisha was Elijah's disciple and heir in prophecy. His life
story can be read in 2 Kings 2:1–13:21. Finally, the Gemara finishes
its commentary to the Mishnah (p. 166, line 10–p. 167, line 11).
You might want to flip back to page 111 and review the Mishnah
to refresh your memory.[24]

*Congratulations! If you studied this entire passage, you have en-
countered almost every type of material in the Gemara:* Mishnah,
Baraita, Aggadah *(stories about the sages) and* Midrash *(expositions of Biblical verses). You might even want to have a party at
the conclusion of such a long passage. Rejoice! You are a student
of Talmud.*

16. SPIRITUALIZING THE CONCRETE: WHAT IS A HOUSE?

Bava Metzia 101b
Volume VI, page 111, line 7–page 114, line 2
Difficulty Factor: 1

*This passage shows one of the sages' propensities: to take a con-
crete item and highlight its spiritual aspect. This would be an especially good passage for those who are moving from one location*

---

24. There is so much in this passage that relates to psychology and mysticism. You might want to have a mental health professional study this passage
with you to shed light on it from that perspective. You might also want to look
at Rabbi Steinsaltz's *The Thirteen Petalled Rose* (see the For Further Reading
section), particularly pages 60–61, to see how the characters in this story relate
to the mystical *sefirot*.

to another to study because it makes us think about the definition of a home, what we put into it, and what we get out of it, both physically and spiritually.

What is a house for rent? According to the Mishnah, it is one set of concrete parts of a building. The Gemara takes the Mishnah's concrete definition and focuses on the spiritual aspect of it, that is, the mezuzah on the door of such a building.

However, first the Gemara, on page 112, lines 3–5, clarifies the distinction made in the Mishnah between what a tenant must do and what a landlord must do. This is quite different from what we would consider a tenant's obligations to be today. However, the principle is the same: today, if a skilled worker is needed to make the repairs (e.g., plumber, electrician), then the landlord provides it. If a skilled worker is not needed (e.g., replacing a lightbulb), the tenant is responsible.

Then the Gemara (p. 112, line 6–p. 114, line 2) addresses a problem we frequently face in our mobile society: if you are moving out of an apartment, do you leave the mezuzah or take it with you? The answer provided in law and lore here is clear: if we rented from a non-Jew or we know the apartment will be occupied by a non-Jew, we take the mezuzah. However, if a Jew is the next tenant, or is likely to be, then we leave the mezuzah.

What role does the mitzvah of mezuzah play in your life? Or, better put, how do you physically remind yourself each day of your connection to the one God of Judaism? When bad fortune befalls you, do you check your mezuzot? Does a mezuzah protect a person by its very presence? We have a passage from the Yerushalmi that suggests that it might do so.

Ardavan [the Fifth] sent our holy rabbi [Judah the Patriarch] a fine, priceless pearl, and said to him, "Send me something as valuable as this!" [So Rabbi] sent him a mezuzah. [Ardavan] said to him, "I sent you an item whose price cannot be fixed, but you sent me something worth but one *follarion!*" [Rabbi] said to him, "Your possessions and my possessions [all added together] are not equivalent [to a single word of the Torah]. Moreover, you sent me something that I must guard [and protect from theft, namely, the pearl]. But I sent you something that will guard you while you sleep! As it is stated [in Scripture], 'When you walk, it [Torah] will lead you; [when you lie down, it will watch over you]'" (Proverbs 6:22). (*Pe'ah* 1:1, 16d; *The Talmud of the Land of Israel, Volume 2: Pe'ah*, p. 60)

Here we see the tension between rationalist and mystical (some would say, superstitious) thinking. Most sages would probably urge the observance of the mitzvah of mezuzah because it is written in the Torah. Yet other sages seem to suggest that this mitzvah benefits the doer and that failing to observe this mitzvah can have dire consequences. Both views can probably be experienced as true at different times. Does connection with God (as embodied in having a mezuzah) make you feel safer? How?[25]

17. CONCRETIZING THE SPIRITUAL: WHAT IS A BLESSING?

Bava Metzia 107a
Volume VI, page 197, line 4–page 202, line 14
Difficulty Factor: 1

Here we see another propensity of the sages: to take spiritual matters and concretize and quantify them. "But wait a minute!" you might say. "You just said the sages have a propensity to spiritualize the concrete. Now you're telling me they concretize the spiritual." And I'd say, "Exactly! The sages feel that material things have spiritual aspects and spiritual things have material aspects. Aren't the sages incredible!"

This passage is an extensive exploration of the promise made by God to the Jewish people in Deuteronomy:

And it shall come to pass, because you hearken to these ordinances, and keep, and do them, that the Lord your God shall keep with you the covenant and the mercy which He swore unto your fathers, and He will love you and bless you and multiply you; He will also bless the fruit of your body and the fruit of your land, your corn and your wine and your oil, the increase of your kine and the young

---

25. If you really want a sense of accomplishment, read tractate *Mezuzah*—yes, a whole tractate! It's one of the minor tractates of the Talmud and it's very, very short. Incidentally, the laws about mezuzot it contains are quite interesting.

of your flock, in the land which He swore unto your fathers to give you. You shall be blessed above all the peoples; there shall not be male or female barren among you, or among your cattle. And the Lord will take away from you all sickness. (Deuteronomy 7:12–15)

The Gemara here will explore this passage in detail. Just as the sages often felt the urge to emphasize the spiritual of the physical realm, they likewise wanted to explore the physical aspects of spiritual phenomena. The Torah promises blessings, but what exactly, in operational terms, are blessings? You might be surprised at the very concrete, physical answer some sages give to this question. To be blessed is to be able to easily and conveniently satisfy one's physical needs and ambitions. This being the Talmud, though, such simple definitions of a blessing are not allowed to stand unaugmented.

For example, it can be a blessing, on the one hand, to be close to a synagogue. On the other hand, we can gain merit by traveling a distance to a synagogue. In other words, as with almost everything else in the Talmud, there are positives and negatives to be found in each issue. Note, please, that the person who gains merit for going to a synagogue to pray (p. 198, line 7) is a woman. In fact, the passage on page 198, line 7, is well worth studying separately since it shows that women prayed beautifully in those days, even though we have relatively few recorded episodes of their having done so.

Our Rabbis taught: A maiden who gives herself up to prayer, [and] a gadabout widow . . . behold these bring destruction upon the world. But it is not so; for Rabbi Yoḥanan has said: We learned fear of sin from a maiden [who gave herself up to prayer] and [confidence in] the bestowal of reward from a [gadabout] widow!

Fear of sin from a maiden—for Rabbi Yoḥanan heard a maiden fall upon her face and exclaim, "Lord of the Universe! You have created paradise and Gehinnom; You have created righteous and wicked. May it be Your will that men should not stumble through me."

[Confidence in] the bestowal of reward from a widow—a certain widow had a synagogue in her neighborhood; yet she used to come daily to the School of Rabbi Yoḥanan and pray there. He said to her, "My daughter, is there not a synagogue in your neighborhood?" She answered him, "Rabbi, but have I not the reward for the steps!" (*Sotah* 22a)

This passage shows how the Gemara could take materials from earlier generations and turn them on their heads. This whole Gemara passage in *Sotah* is a comment to that Mishnah that can so anger some readers, in which Rabbi Eliezer declares that anyone who teaches his daughter Torah teaches her lewdness (*Sotah* 20a). This Mishnah goes on to say that a foolish pietist and a female pharisee, among others, bring destruction upon the world. As an elaboration of that one category of women, the female pharisee, the Bavli brings the Baraita about which sorts of women bring destruction on the world. Then, in its characteristic way, the Bavli immediately shows that women pray faithfully and save the world from destruction. The sages learned fear of sin from a young maiden and confidence in a Divine reward from a widow. This is a typical case of the Gemara contrasting theory with real life and the real-life case the sages bring supporting what the sages wanted to emphasize, that is, that women don't destroy the world.

Beginning on page 199, line 7, we have a long passage about medicine as it was practiced in those days. As with so many other things in the Talmud, a great gulf of time and practice separates us from the medicine of those days.

It is not at all unusual to see large sections of medical information in the Babylonian Talmud. Some of it is remarkably similar to ancient medicine as practiced in other cultures at that time. For example, contrast the teachings about the wind (p. 200, lines 1–9) and these teachings of Hippocrates:

> South winds induce dullness of hearing, dimness of visions, heaviness of the head, torpor, and languor; when these prevail, such symptoms occur in diseases. (Aphorisms 3:5)

> If the winter be southerly, raining, and calm, but the spring dry and northerly, women whose term of delivery should be in Spring have abortions from any slight cause; and those who reach their full time bring forth children who are feeble and diseased, so that they either die presently or, if they live, are puny and unhealthy. (Aphorisms 3:12)

I would allow some of this material in the Talmud to pass right over your head if it is too difficult now. However, on page 201, starting on line 7, we can note that one thing, at least, has remained constant: breakfast eaters are winners.

At the bottom of page 202, lines 8–14, we find a prescription for a wholesome life that could still stand today: pray and eat regularly. In other words, nourish your soul and your body. What is a life of blessing? It is a life of physical and spiritual fulfillment. The sages do not advocate asceticism, overintellectualism, or a life devoted to acquiring material goods only. A life of blessing is a life of balance and wholeness.[26]

18. WHO IS NEEDY?

Bava Metzia **111a–b**
Volume VI, page 259, line 7–page 265, line 9
Difficulty Factor: 5

If for passage #11 you thought you heard the theme music for The Twilight Zone, *then the theme music for this passage might be* Mission: Impossible. *But take heart! If you treat yourself with enough patience you'll make your way through the material quite nicely. This passage is especially important because it deals with interpersonal ethics and how important it is to make timely payments.*

This passage, a Mishnah with some Gemara to it, is quite difficult because we must juggle many different dimensions in our minds to understand the fine distinctions the text is making. Let's come to grips with them one by one and then try to put the whole thing together like a three-dimensional chess game.

One of the first things we must recognize is that we have here a melding of different Midrashic traditions on the following Torah verses, which state the same idea in different ways. (By now, this should send you a signal that the sages will have a field day exploring the differences and similarities between the two.)

---

26. You might want to have a physician or nurse contrast and compare the medical theories of the Talmud with medical thought today as you read through this passage.

> You shall not oppress a hired servant that is poor and needy, whether he be of your brethren or your strangers that are in your land within your gates. In the same day you shall give him his hire, neither shall the sun go down upon it; for he is poor and sets his heart upon it; lest he cry against you unto the Lord and it be sin in you. (Deuteronomy 24:14–15)

> You shall not oppress your neighbor, nor rob him; the wages of a hired servant shall not abide with you all night until the morning. (Leviticus 19:13)

These are two verses from the Torah that mandate timely payment of a wage or rental fee. The verse in Deuteronomy commands you positively to pay on time and the verse in Leviticus prohibits you from delaying payment, that is, it is a negative commandment, a prohibition. So we have this mitzvah as both a positive and a negative commandment. This is relevant because there are different consequences for violating positive and negative commandments.

Note the difference in the language between these two verses. The passage from Deuteronomy includes many categories of persons in its rule. The verse from Leviticus does not. This is what the Mishnah is referring to when it differentiates between one group and another and which verse might be applied to it. Who are the categories of persons referred to in the verses from Deuteronomy? They are Jews, non-Jews, converts to Judaism, and resident aliens. The last group are non-Jews who live in Israel who observe some of the practices of Judaism (see *ger toshav*, p. 177, column 1, 2nd entry in the *Reference Guide*) but who do not eat kosher foods. While there is no hard and fast definition of what this category of persons must observe, most authorities agree that they observe the seven Noachide laws: the prohibitions of idolatry, blasphemy, bloodshed, sexual sins, theft, and eating from a living animal, as well as the injunction to establish a legal system (*Tosefta, Avodah Zarah* 8:4). These laws were given to the generations of the flood, that is, before Jews existed. They are deemed mandatory for all human beings.

The Midrash on Deuteronomy 24:14–15 systematically explores the verses:

"You shall not oppress a hired servant that is poor and needy" (Deuteronomy 24:14): Does not Scripture say elsewhere, "Nor rob him" (Leviticus 19:13)? Why then does it say here, "You shall not oppress"? Because you learn therefrom that if one withholds the wages of a hired servant, he transgresses four negative commandments, to wit:

1. "You shall not oppress" (Leviticus 19:13),
2. "Nor rob" (Leviticus 19:13),
3. "The wages . . . shall not abide with you all night" (Leviticus 19:13) and
4. "In the same day you shall give him his hire, neither shall the sun go down upon it" (Deuteronomy 24:15).

"[For he is poor], and sets his heart upon it" (Deuteronomy 24:15): I conclude therefrom that this applies only to work that he sets his heart upon; what about work which he does not set his heart upon, such as carding and combing [flax]? The verse states, "You shall not oppress" (Deuteronomy 24:14)—in any kind of work.

"[That is poor and needy]": I conclude that this applies only to a workman who is poor and needy. What about any other workman? The verse states, "You shall not oppress"—any workman, [whether needy or not]. If so, why does Scripture say "poor and needy"? Because I requite the cause of a poor and needy workman more quickly than that of any other person.

"Of your brethren"—but not of others—"or of your strangers" (Deuteronomy 24:14): This refers to the righteous proselyte, showing that in his case one transgresses two negative commandments. Rabbi Yose ben Rabbi Yehudah says: [He transgresses] only the commandment not to oppress.

["Within your gates" (Deuteronomy 24:14): This is the resident alien. I conclude therefrom that this applies only to the wages of a hired man. What about the wages of a hired animal or of hired tools? The verse states, "That are in your land" (Deuteronomy 24:14)—anything (hired) in your land.] (*Sifrei* Deuteronomy *Piska* 278)

The Midrash on Leviticus 19:13 likewise systematically explores its Torah verse:

"The wages of one that is hired shall not reside with you [over-night] till morning" (Leviticus 19:13). I do not have here [anything but] the wage of a person. The wage of an animal and an imple-ment, where do they come from? The wage of [a piece of] land, where does it come from? Scripture says, "The wage shall not re-main overnight," [i.e.], the wage of anything.

"Until morning" (Leviticus 19:13). [The employer] does not transgress this [precept of timely payment of wages] until the first morning. It is possible that even if he came and demanded it, Scrip-ture did not say "with you," but it should not remain [overnight] with you intentionally. It could be that even if [the wage] is signed over to a shopkeeper or money changer, he may make a claim for it. Scripture says "with you"; it should not stay [overnight] with you intentionally.

"The wage should not remain with you overnight until morn-ing." I do not have [here] anything but the hire of a day [worker] that is collected all night. The wage of a night [worker] that is col-lected all day, from whence do I know [that this verse applies to it also]? Scripture says, "On that day you shall give him his wage." (Deuteronomy 24:14). (*Sifra* Leviticus on Leviticus 19:13)

Everything should be pretty clear to this point. The verses them-selves are straightforward and the Midrash passages explore each phrase of the verses, relating the law to the Torah and connect-ing these two verses from Deuteronomy and Leviticus to each other. What's going to happen is that the editor of the Gemara is going to try to put these Midrashic traditions, and some other traditions, together. Obviously, they were not originally intended to be melded together; they were meant to stand on their own.

Our passage consists of a Mishnah, which is essentially the same as a Baraita, from the school of Rabbi Ishmael, and the two Midrash passages come from the school of Rabbi Akiva. (Rabbi Yehudah, Rabbi Yose's father, was a pupil of Rabbi Akiva and we presume the son continued in his father's tradition.) These two schools repre-sent diametrically opposing approaches to the Torah. Rabbi Akiva's school, as should be obvious from the Midrash passages above, believed in expounding every word of the Torah separately. Rabbi Ishmael's school believed in reading the Torah in a straightforward, rational way as opposed to Rabbi Akiva's more fanciful method. So what we have in our Gemara passage is really the opposition of

	Does This Precept Apply?	
	Positive (Deuteronomy)	Negative (Leviticus)
Mishnah (Rabbi Ishmael)		
Jew	doesn't say	doesn't say
Non-Jew	doesn't say	doesn't say
Convert	doesn't say	doesn't say
Resident Alien	doesn't say	doesn't say
Worker's Wage	yes	yes
Animal's Rental	yes	yes
Implement's Rental	yes	yes
Baraita (*Sifrei* to Deuteronomy, Rabbi Akiva)		
Jew	yes	doesn't say
Non-Jew	no	doesn't say
Convert	yes	doesn't say
Resident Alien	yes	doesn't say
Worker's Wage	yes	doesn't say
Animal's Rental	yes	doesn't say
Implement's Rental	yes	doesn't say
Rabbi Yose the son of Rabbi Yehudah (Rabbi Akiva)		
Jew	doesn't say	doesn't say
Non-Jew	doesn't say	doesn't say
Convert	yes	doesn't say
Resident Alien	yes	no
Worker's Wage	doesn't say	doesn't say (yes)
Animal's Rental	no	yes
Implement's Rental	no	yes
Baraita of the School of Rabbi Ishmael		
Jew	doesn't say	doesn't say
Non-Jew	doesn't say	doesn't say
Convert	doesn't say	doesn't say
Resident Alien	yes	no
Worker's Wage	yes	yes
Animal's Rental	yes	yes
Implement's Rental	yes	yes

two schools of thought on two very important Torah texts. The table on page 109 might help demonstrate these views.

If this is too difficult, just let it go over your head and move on. Don't become frustrated or stuck on something you can come back to when you know more.

As the Gemara juggles all these texts, you might feel something akin to the intricacy (and/or frustration) of trying to get slightly different computer programs to run simultaneously on your computer. Many of the concepts you find in this passage are similar to American legal concepts: there is a statute of limitations, so to speak, on when the worker can ask for his wages and there is even something like a "company store" (p. 260, lines 2–3). There are differences between employment practices then and now. Perhaps the closest we can come to understanding this passage is to think of the case of migrant workers or day laborers working for a contractor who wish to be paid immediately after their day of work is over.

On page 263, line 8, some of the discrepancies between these passages are solved by referring to a *gezerah shavah* (p. 150, column 1, 1st entry in the *Reference Guide*). This is a method of Torah interpretation whereby the same word or phrase is used in two separate places and analogies are drawn between them based on their common use of this one word. Here the word *s'khir*, "hired worker," is used in the two texts, and an analogy can therefore be drawn between them. However, Rabbi Yose does not agree with this analogy, and indeed, one should be careful in using this technique. For example, if you hear a physician being referred to as "doctor," you might think that all "doctors" are physicians. But this will lead you into trouble when you find out that "doctors" are also dentists, professors, and, occasionally, basketball players.

On pages 264–265 we find a very fine distinction between poor and needy. In essence, a poor person still has dignity, while the sages portray a needy person as without shame. Do you agree with the Gemara's ruling (p. 265, line 9) that a poor person should be paid before a needy one? Is it best to reward a person who has dignity before one without dignity? Be sure to read the Concepts and Notes entries on page 265; they shed some needed light on this topic.

19. THE FRAGRANCE OF THE WORLD TO COME

Bava Metzia 114a
Volume VI, page 302, lines 1–9
Difficulty Factor: 1

Are you feeling as if the Talmud is incredibly vast and your inexperience makes you incapable of understanding it? Then read this passage! It shows how even great sages could feel this way and the lengths to which God went to make it possible for them to study.

This is a short passage that should provide some comfort for those who are just beginning to study Talmud. It is about a famous sage, Rabbah bar Avuha, and the prophet Elijah. Elijah was thought to wander the world and is often depicted as speaking to the sages. Our story may explain how Rabbah bar Avuha became, suddenly, a man of wealth and power. Indeed, it seems rather clear from our sources (e.g., *Gittin* 31b and *Ḥullin* 124a) that Rabbah bar Avuha held a high position in the Jewish secular power structure of his day. Elsewhere he is portrayed as having talked with Elijah (*Megillah* 15b).

Rabbah bar Avuha, in talking with Elijah, tells the prophet that he can barely master the four orders of the Mishnah that are usually studied. The six orders of the Mishnah are as follows:

1. Seeds (*Zeraim*): Rules about Agriculture, e.g., all the tithes discussed in the Introduction.
2. Seasons (*Moed*): Shabbat and the Holidays.
3. Women (*Nashim*): Marriage, Divorce, etc. *Ketubot* is in this order.
4. Damages (*Nezikin*): Civil and Criminal laws. *Bava Metzia* is in this order.
5. Holy Things (*Kodashim*): Kashrut and the laws of the sacrifices.
6. Purities (*Teharot*): Rules of ritual purity and impurity.

Rabbah bar Avuha claims that he cannot study the first four tractates (alternately, the middle four), let alone the other two, because he does not have enough money to support himself and give him the free time to study.

This passage is interesting because of the potential it has to give us a glimpse at the history of a well-known sage. As you know by now, not every legend that was ever told about a sage made it into the Gemara. Why was this story included? What needed explaining that it explained? Could it have been an explanation of Rabbah bar Avuha's sudden wealth? Or an explanation of why he did not seem to be too learned at one point in his career? Or an explanation of why he gave his sons-in-law so much wealth? (One of his sons-in-law, Rav Naḥman, married his daughter Yalta and was a well-known sage.) Did people wonder about whence came the power and wealth of this family and see this as the explanation? If so, many of us could do worse than to have as the source of our prosperity the scent of the World to Come.

There is a practical lesson for us in this. If our goal is study of Talmud and observance of mitzvot, this story implies that God will provide us with the means necessary to live while we study. We can always make excuses why we cannot study. Everyone has pressing time commitments. However, as Rabbi Tarfon says (*Avot* 2:20), "The day is short; the task is great; the workmen are lazy; the reward is great; and the Master of the house is insistent." This same sage would also say, "You are not required to complete the work [of Torah study], but you are not free to evade it" (*Avot* 2:21). If we take these words to heart and seek out the scent of the World to Come, we will see the fulfillment of our tasks.[27]

20. WEDDINGS AND FUNERALS

Ketubot 7b–8b
Volume VII, page 84, line 8–page 105, line 4
Difficulty Factor: 5

If you are interested in Jewish liturgy, ritual, and custom, then this is the passage for you. There is more material on these matters here

---

27. If you'd like to read a bit more about Rabbah bar Avuha's encounters with Elijah, just flip back to page 299, line 10. The problems he and Elijah discuss are rather technical and were therefore not included in this passage. However, you might want to come back to this material after you have a little more experience.

than in any other passage in this volume. This segment of the Talmud is about consecrating moments of transition and concentrates on weddings and funerals.

This passage involves experiences most of us have had: eating, blessing, wedding, and mourning. Before looking at this passage, some background information will help to make it understandable. Before you open *Ketubot*, let's briefly go over the etiquette of weddings and funerals 1,500 years ago, a sort of ancient Miss Manners. You can read the following descriptions and/or look up these entries in the *Reference Guide*:

Aveilut: page 158, column 1, 3rd entry
Birkat HaMazon: page 173, column 1, 5th entry
Birkat Hatanim: page 173, column 2, 1st entry
Erusin: page 161, column 2, 4th entry
Kiddushin: page 253, column 1, 1st entry
Kinyan sudar: page 254, column 2, 2nd entry
Kos shel brakhah: page 203, column 1, 4th entry
Minyan: page 220, column 1, 3rd entry
Mi'un: page 215, column 1, 1st entry
Nissu'in: page 229, column 2, 3rd entry
Panim Hadashot: page 245, column 1, 6th entry
Shurah: page 264, column 1, 4th entry

What was a wedding in ancient days? It was a good bit like a Jewish wedding is now.[28] First of all, what we now do in the course of one ceremony was two ceremonies in the sages' day. There was the betrothal and then, much later, the actual wedding. For example, a girl could be betrothed (i.e., engaged) at the age of three and not married until the age of fourteen. Today, the betrothal and the wedding go together since this ancient arrangement caused various problems. (For example, a betrothed woman who wished to break her engagement required a divorce, and being a divorcee could cause problems for a woman.) The betrothal could be accomplished either by giving the woman money

---

28. In fact, you might want to look at a videotape of a Jewish wedding and watch as all the parts of the ritual unfold.

or its equivalent (e.g., a ring), by giving her a document, or by having sexual intercourse with her. However, this last form of betrothal was forbidden long ago since it could lead to obvious problems. Betrothal was known as *kiddushin* or *erusin*.

Part of the betrothal process was the wedding document, the ketubah. In ancient days, long before the Rabbinic era, a husband would pay a price for a bride. Eventually, instead of having to pay this money "up front," it was written into the wedding contract as a lien against the man's property in case of divorce. This had two beneficial effects: (1) it meant that even poor men could marry and (2) it meant that a man had to have money to divorce and that this money would go to the wife as financial support after the divorce. In other words, every couple had a prenuptial agreement and a divorce decree written at the time of the wedding. This was advantageous to women, since the divorce decree was determined when the man wanted her the most, not, as we do it in America, at the time of divorce, when he wants her the least. You might want to look at a ketubah, many of which are beautiful artworks today, to see what one says. In the traditional ketubah, a man agrees to provide his wife with food, clothing, and sexual relations. Other, additional financial agreements can be written into the ketubah and we have some evidence that there was competition to make the ketubah, that is, the amount promised to the woman, as large as possible (see B. Bava Metzia 104b). The ketubah belongs to the woman. She (or her agent) acquires this document in a ceremony called *kinyan sudar*. The groom symbolically exchanges a handkerchief for the ketubah.

The actual wedding of the couple takes place under a *huppah*, a wedding canopy. (Today, the betrothal takes place there, too.) The wedding ceremony is called Birkat Hatanim ("groom's blessing") or nissu'in ("marriage"). As you'll note in our passage, the Talmud refers to six "groom's blessings" while the blessings said at a wedding are often called "*sheva berakhot*," the seven blessings. The discrepancy is reconciled in that a blessing is said over the wine at the wedding, in addition to the six groom's blessings. After these seven blessings have been recited and the couple has drunk the wine over which the blessing was said, the glass is broken and a festive meal follows.

In Judaism, after we eat a meal, we say the grace after meals, called Birkat HaMazon.[29] The first part of this grace is called *zimmun*, "invitation" and is a call-and-response formula that invites everyone present to thank God for the meal. This *zimmun* has special forms for weddings, circumcisions, and a house of mourning. In other words, the feelings of the people present and the import of the occasion are reflected in this invitation. At a wedding, not only is the *zimmun* augmented to reflect the occasion, but the wedding blessings are added to the Grace itself. The rules about how many days one inserts these additions into the Grace after Meals are taken up in this passage. Certainly they are recited for the first seven days after the wedding. In ancient days, and in traditional circles to this day, the wedding couple would be feted in their friends' houses for the first week after their wedding. This is entirely reasonable: they introduce themselves as a new couple to their whole circle of friends. This marks a sensible tendency in Judaism: we celebrate only after something has been accomplished. Rather than giving wedding showers before a nuptial that may or may not take place, we wait until after the "deal is done," so to speak, to celebrate.

One of the things that may surprise a new student of the Talmud is how fluid rituals seem to have been in the Rabbinic era. One sage prays one way and another a different way and both these ways can be right. "Creative liturgy" is nothing new. In fact, it has its roots in the Talmud. Jewish rituals at life-transition moments tend to be brief. The feelings are so intense and real, as a rule, that very little ritual framework is needed to invoke and encompass them.

As Jews, we often tend to be envious of Christians who can pray extemporaneously, and yet we are ill at ease doing it ourselves. We need not be. It is—or rather, can be—a legitimate form of Jewish prayer. On the other hand, it can lead to problems when the extemporaneous prayer does not seem to suit the occasion. (Such seems to have been the case in the story told on page 99, line 6–page 103, line 7.)

---

29. If you are not familiar with Birkat HaMazon, you might want to take a look at it in a prayer book.

Another thing you'll need to know before you start on this passage is the difference between long and short blessings. You can either read the description here or the one in the Notes section on page 91. Short blessings are the ones with which you are probably most familiar, such as the blessings over bread and wine. They have the "Blessed are You, Lord our God, Ruler of the Universe . . ." formula. Long blessings have this formula at the beginning and a similar one at the end. What we might call "in-between" blessings do not start with the formula but end with it and are usually part of a series of blessings. The following are examples of each sort of blessing in turn:

1. Short: Blessed are You, Lord our God, Ruler of the Universe, Creator of the fruit of the vine.

2. Long: Blessed are You, Lord our God, Ruler of the Universe, who has given us a Torah of truth and planted within us everlasting life. Blessed are You, Lord, Giver of the Torah.

3. You favor people with knowledge and teach mortals understanding. Grant us knowledge, understanding, and insight. Praised are You, gracious Giver of Knowledge.

As an exercise, try identifying which of the blessings in this series of blessings after the *Haftarah* reading are long or in-between:

1. Blessed are You, Lord our God, Ruler of the universe, creator of all the worlds, righteous in all generations, faithful God, who says and performs, who speaks and fulfills, for all Your words are true and just. Faithful are you, Lord our God, and faithful are Your words, no word of Yours returns unfulfilled, for You are a faithful and merciful God and King. Blessed are You, O Lord our God, who are faithful in all Your words.

2. Have compassion on Zion, for it is the source of our life; save the humbled soul speedily in our days. Blessed are You, O Lord, who makes Zion rejoice in her children.

3. Gladden us, Lord our God, with the appearance of Your servant Elijah the prophet, and with the rule of the house of David Your anointed. May he soon come and bring joy to our heart. Let no stranger occupy David's throne; let others no longer possess themselves of his glory, for You did promise him by Your holy name that his light would never go out. Blessed are You, O Lord, shield of David.

4. We thank You for the Torah, for the worship, for the prophets, and for this Sabbath day, which You have given us, Lord our God, for holiness and rest, for glory and beauty. We thank and bless You, Lord our God, for all things; be Your name ever blessed by every living being. Blessed are You, O Lord, who hallows the Sabbath.
(Answers: (1) is long; (2), (3), and (4) are in-between.)

How did God create humanity? This becomes an important issue in our passage. As you probably know, there are two different creation stories in the Torah and the way humanity's creation is described in these passages is strikingly different.

> And God said: Let us make man in our image, after our likeness; and let them have dominion over the fish of the sea, and over the fowl of the air, and over the cattle, and over all the earth, and over every creeping thing that creeps upon the earth. And God created man in His own image, in the image of God created He him; male and female created He them. (Genesis 1:26–27)

In this version, man and woman are created together, at the same time. In the next version (the one with the snake) Adam is created first:

> Then the Lord God formed man of the dust of the ground, and breathed into his nostrils the breath of life; and man became a living soul. . . . And the Lord God said: It is not good that the man should be alone; I will make a helpmeet for him. . . . And the Lord God caused a deep sleep to fall upon the man, and he slept; and He took one of his ribs, and closed up the place with flesh instead thereof. And the rib, which the Lord God had taken from the man,

made He woman, and brought her unto the man. (Genesis 2:7, 18, 21–22)

For a fuller comparison, you might want to read Genesis, chapters 1–2, in their entirety.

An issue the Gemara brings up is that of "new faces." To understand this concept, imagine you are, as so often happens these days, attending a weekend full of wedding festivities at which new guests are continually arriving and augmenting the sense of happiness (and tension!). That is what this concept is referring to. As each set of new guests arrive, it changes the dynamic of the party and, according to the practice outlined in the Talmud, this is consecrated by saying a special form of the Grace after Meals.

Consider the similarities between weddings and funerals, since these two events are juxtaposed (p. 96, line 5–p. 103, line 7). They are moments of transition when large family gatherings take place that center on a brief ritual ceremony, great emotion, and a meal that has a ceremonial quality to it. They are also moments of tension, since members of the wedding or funeral parties may behave in untoward ways that are memorialized in family lore forever after.[30]

Today, we might be shocked when reading that so much wine was to be drunk after a funeral, as suggested on page 104. Wine then was a far more dilute and less alcoholic beverage than wine is today. It was made the way tea is still made in Russia. A little strong tea is poured into the bottom of the cup and then diluted with hot water from the samovar. Similarly, a strong wine concentrate was poured into a cup and then diluted with water. Think whiskey and water rather than whiskey neat. In addition, drinking wine after it was blessed was seen as a way of imbibing God's essence and thus a way of augmenting holiness.[31]

---

30. After reading this section, you may want to discuss how we deal with feelings of guilt and anger after the death of a loved one.

31. You might want to have a member of your local Jewish burial society (Ḥevrah Kaddisha) show you the shrouds in which Jews are buried to this day. Taking responsibility for burying Jews properly is a great mitzvah, and the persons involved in this process can probably enlighten you greatly about it.

21. TRUTH OR TACT?

Ketubot 16b–17b
Volume VIII, page 27, line 8–page 36, line 3
Difficulty Factor: 1

How do personality, financial position, and tact come together to affect behavior? These are the deep issues at the heart of this passage. Because these are timeless concerns, it will be very easy to draw parallels between much of what people are reported to have done in this passage and the way people behave today. That makes this passage very easy to understand.

To tell the truth or to be socially correct, that is the question addressed in this passage. It also asks another question that is important today: How much of our standard behavior should we abandon at a celebration?

It will be necessary to know about Bet (the House of) Shammai and Bet Hillel to understand this passage. You can look up the following entries in the *Reference Guide*:

Kulei Bet Shammai v'humrei Bet Hillel: page 251, column 2, entry 2[32]
Seder hadei'ot: page 95, column 1, entry 1

Bet Shammai tended to represent the interests of the upper classes while Bet Hillel tended to represent the poorer classes. The law is almost always decided according to Bet Hillel, although Bet Shammai's opinions are mentioned as important and as a valid expression of a different point of view. As you read the material on pages 27–28, you can see why it makes sense for Bet Hillel, speaking from a position of poverty, to express its opinion. A poor bride associated with Bet Hillel might not have the most beautiful dress or have had access to a diet or medical care

---

32. If you have *The Book of Legends*, edited by Hayim Bialik and Yehoshua Ravnitzky and translated by William Braude (New York: Schocken, 1992), you can find more information about them on pages 208–209, entries #31–33. In general, this is a resource well worth learning how to use. If you wish to follow neither of those courses, read on.

that would produce the greatest beauty. Nonetheless, *every* bride is to be praised as beautiful. The brides associated with Bet Shammai would have been more likely to have had the advantages that would produce beauty, and so Bet Shammai might have felt no need to say anything but the truth about its brides. In almost every case, the law follows Bet Hillel over Bet Shammai. (Jewish law is quite democratic in its values.)

This passage illustrates an important concept found over and over again in the Talmud, that is, values are rarely absolutes but are balanced, one against the other. Here, truth telling and social harmony are balanced against each other. In this situation, social harmony is deemed more important than truth telling. It is probably easy to think of moments in your own life when these two values came into conflict. At those times, did you follow Bet Shammai or Bet Hillel?

On page 29, lines 1–4, we learn how a great sage used to sing to the bride. Rav Dimi, like many other sages, would travel from the Land of Israel to Babylonia in order to teach the Babylonians about the customs practiced there. Today, we would call Rav Dimi a scholar in residence on a guest lectureship.

We also learn on page 29, lines 9–14, that rabbis were apparently not universally loved in those days, as today they are not, either. Some were admired by the public for their learning and piety, while others were "incompetent and worthless pseudo-scholars." It is somewhat reassuring to know that then, as now, people loved and hated their rabbis and were quick to praise and criticize them. I'm sure some rabbis would like people to follow Bet Hillel and praise them no matter how poorly they do. However, it seems that the people followed Bet Shammai in this regard and told the truth about their rabbis.

On page 30, line 4–page 31, line 4, we read a fanciful story about Rav Shmuel bar Yitzhak. The sticks he is described as dancing with might remind us of the lulav we shake on Sukkot and the dancing and happiness associated with that holiday. When we read, as we often will, about supernatural events connected with the sages, we must remember that these events were related to the sages' holiness and Torah learning. They were not mere tricks but had deep religious significance that were related to the Torah.

Just as today we often look to science to change the course of events, so then did people look to Torah and prayer to change the course of events.

This story, and the others on page 31, lines 5–12, point to another truth about the sages in those days: everything they did was scrutinized. They were role models and the way they danced was as important as the laws they taught. Here, we find that the sages rejoiced with great abandon at weddings and that this apparently caused some consternation in some individuals. Today, many families, who are otherwise modest in their expenditures, bankrupt themselves to hold lavish Bar and Bat Mitzvah parties or wedding receptions. We might ask where we should draw the line between appropriate, joyous celebration and wretched excess. This passage seems to support those who would rejoice greatly at such happy times. Of course, there is a difference between rejoicing and simply displaying one's wealth.

From here (p. 32, line 1) to the end of the passage (p. 36, line 3), we study the relative importance of wedding processions, funeral processions (especially the funerals of sages), and kings' processions by examining which one takes precedence in the public domain. In general, the living take precedence over the dead and their moments of transition take precedence over Torah study; all the more so does the funeral procession (and we would assume, the wedding) of a Torah scholar take precedence over Torah study. In other words, study is important but people come first.

Agrippa I (10 B.C.E.–44 C.E.) was king of Judea from 41 to 44 C.E. His three-year reign was a relatively good time for the Jews of Judea. He was sympathetic to the Pharisees and observed Jewish precepts. We should be quite careful about assuming the historicity of stories in the Talmud. While the story about Agrippa (p. 32, lines 4–5) might be true, it could equally as well be a legend that was attached to his name and character later. If this were the case, it would not diminish the importance of this story but simply change the way we understand and value it.

One final note about this entire passage: It is remarkable how much physicality we encounter in these texts—the bride's appearance, the energetic dancing, the juggling, the public procession for funerals. We have been called the People of the Book, but Judaism is a religion of body as well as spirit. Physical expressions of religious intentions are important, as this passage shows. We have bodies and they must be made a part of our relationship with God and the mitzvot.

22. "WHO IS A JEW?" AND "CONSEQUENCES OF INAPPROPRIATE SEXUAL INTERCOURSE"

Ketubot 29a
Volume IX, page 3, line 1–page 7, line 5
Difficulty Factor: 5

> *This passage is not for the squeamish. In fact, you might want to delay studying this passage until the end of your first course of study. This chapter of tractate* Ketubot *deals with what happens when men and women come together in ways that are incorrect and what the consequences of this behavior are. The sages' conceptions of sexuality, relationships, compensation for sexual transgressions, and divisions within the Jewish community may seem very foreign at first. If you are willing to take the time to stand in the sages' shoes and really understand what they were doing, this passage will probably strike a familiar chord in you.*

We will study the first Mishnah in this chapter along with a tiny bit of the Gemara to it. Even given such a short section, you will need a great deal of background to understand it. Therefore, I suggest the following preparation.

1. **Read the Introduction** to Chapter Three in this volume.

2. **Read the following sections** of the Torah:

And if a man entice a virgin that is not betrothed, and lie with her, he shall surely pay a dowry for her to be his wife. If her father utterly refuse to give her unto him, he shall pay money according to the dowry of virgins. (Exodus 22:15–16)

If a man find a damsel that is a virgin, that is not betrothed, and lay hold on her and lie with her, and they be found, then the man that lay with her shall give unto the damsel's father fifty shekels of silver and she shall be his wife, because he has humbled her; he may not put her away all his days. (Deuteronomy 22:28–29)

You might also want to read Leviticus 18:3–19 and Leviticus 20: 11–14, which are long lists of forbidden sexual relations.

3. You will also need to know the stages a girl goes through in terms of her legal identity in the sages' system. From birth to twelve years, she is called a *ketanah*, a minor, and cannot take legal action for herself (neither can a boy, for that matter). From twelve to twelve-and-a-half (i.e., puberty) she is considered a *na'arah*, a young girl, and her father maintains some authority over her. From twelve-and-a-half on, she is called a *bogeret*, an adult woman, and her father can no longer make decisions on her behalf. You might want to look up the following words in the *Reference Guide*:

Bogeret: page 166, column 1, last entry
Katan/Ketanah: page 252, column 1, 2nd and 3rd entries
Ketubah: page 206, column 2, 2nd entry
Na'arah: page 230, column 2, 4th entry

4. According to Mishnah *Kiddushin* 4:1, ten genealogical groups came from Babylonia to Israel after the first exile (i.e., after the First Temple's destruction in 586 B.C.E.):

People with recognized bloodlines

1. Priests
2. Levites
3. Israelites

People whose bloodlines impair them only with regard to the priesthood

4. *Ḥalalim*: Children of an interdicted priestly union (e.g., between a kohen and a divorcee)

People whose bloodlines are irrelevant

5. Proselytes
6. Freed men

People whose bloodlines are impaired in some way

7. *Mamzerim*: Children of a union forbidden by death or excision
8. *Netinim*: A special group of proselytes, descended from the Gibeonites
9. *Shetuki*: Those who know their mother but not their father
10. Foundling: One who was found in the street and knows neither his father nor his mother

Groups 1, 2, and 3 can marry each other. Groups 2, 3, 4, 5, and 6 can marry each other. Groups 5, 6, 7, and 8 can marry each other. Groups 9 and 10 cannot even marry people in their own group, but they can marry people in categories 5, 6, and 8.

These distinctions may cause contemporary American Jews to sigh wistfully. Most Jewish parents would be happy if their children married Jews, regardless of their bloodlines. By contrast, in ancient days, so important was the purity of a person's bloodline, particularly a priest's, that if a priest married a woman he should not have, the rest of his family cut him off in a public ceremony.[33]

Many of the distinctions made in this Mishnah between types of Jews may seem foreign. However, today we classify Jews in many ways: Reform, Conservative, Orthodox; Israeli and Diaspora; Born Jewish, Converted to Judaism; Frum from Birth, *Ba'al Teshuvah*; and so forth. Each of these labels carries with it certain connotations, justified or not. The classifications in this passage served a similar function in the Rabbinic era.

We, as Americans, may find this categorization scheme particularly difficult to understand. We rebel at the thought that what one's parents, or even distant ancestors, did can affect what one can do in life. Think about it in terms of the British royal family

---

33. You can find the description of this ceremony in Volume VIII, *Ketubot* Part II, pages 267–268. The passage itself can be read on page 268, lines 1–6, but the Notes entry, which begins at the bottom of 267, is quite important to read in order to understand this ritual.

and whom they can marry. That might give you a handle on this system of lineage as a classification tool. As you can see, the goal of the system is keeping the lineage of the priests pure and maintaining a pool of "pure" persons for them to marry. Some interesting questions for discussion or thought are: Does breeding count? What role does your family heritage, genetic or otherwise, play in determining your life?

All these questions of lineage come up because a rapist was required to marry the woman he raped (if she agreed). What if, however, the raped woman came from a category of persons that made her ineligible for marriage with her rapist, for example, if he was a priest and she was a mamzeret? What then? That is the subject of our Mishnah.

The language of our Mishnah is going to sound incredibly cold. However, if you were to read a modern court document assigning a monetary value to human suffering it might sound the same. Given the choice between assigning monetary compensation for suffering and sounding cold, or not compensating the raped woman, we would probably decide, as did the sages, to assign compensation, even if, in the process, it sounds sterile and unfeeling.

5. Read the Background, Concepts, and Notes sections on pages 3–7 *before* reading the text. Then you can read the Translation and Commentary or the Literal Translation.

This passage brings up uncomfortable issues such as "What is incest?" "What is rape?" and "What is seduction?" These issues are in the forefront of American consciousness today. Is the Jewish legal practice of making the transgressor pay a fine better, worse, or simply different than the American legal system? (Remember, in the case in our Mishnah, the fine is paid to the girl's father because she is not legally in her majority. Similarly, in American law, parents often take care of financial transactions for their minor children.) It may be difficult to make the leap from our day to the sages', and a first reading of this passage may make us feel angry. However, after reading it carefully, what we find is that the sages stood squarely on the side of the girl who was violated, and their legislation ensures that she will be taken care of and/or compensated for the hurt done to her by inappropriate sexual intercourse, regardless of her lineage or past experience in life.[34]

23. A JUDAISM THAT RESPONDS TO THE TIMES: THE DICTATES OF USHA

Ketubot 49b–50a
Volume X, page 112, line 9–page 125, line 7
Difficulty Factor: 5

Child support and abandonment. How to give to charity. How to raise children to be menshen. *It sounds like a list of current social issues but it's really the topics addressed in this passage. Obviously, this material is directly applicable to today's world, and this makes it relatively more easily understood.*

The events of world history have a great impact on Judaism. If Judaism had been frozen and rigid, unresponsive to a changing world, then it would have died long ago. It is because Judaism has within it the means to adapt that it has survived.

One of the greatest historical shocks Judaism had to deal with was the double tragedy of the Temple's destruction in 70 C.E. and then the failure of the Bar Kokhba revolt in 135 C.E. The Temple's destruction was a blow to the nation because, until then, the whole system of atonement in Judaism had been predicated on the sacrifice of animals. If you unintentionally committed a sin for which

---

34. You might want to try the following exercise: List all the categories of Jews, or people even peripherally attached to the Jewish people, you can think of. Which of these groups of persons deserve protection against unwanted sexual intercourse under Jewish law? Do you agree, or disagree, with the sages' concept that sexual intercourse before the age of three is irrelevant in terms of the girl's sexual status? (That is, a girl who suffered this experience is still considered a virgin and entitled to the ketubah due a virgin. The assault on her is considered one for which damages would have to be paid. It is simply not categorized as a sexual assault.) If you could argue with the sages, how would you convince them of your point of view?

Consulting a lawyer who knows about sexual assault or harassment might make a useful addition to your discussion; you could contrast Jewish and American law on these topics.

the penalty was death (e.g., lit a fire on Shabbat), then you brought an animal to the Temple and it was killed in your place. In this way, the Temple and its cult were literally lifesaving institutions. Judaism adapted to the loss of the sacrifices by making prayer take their place. Since we could not replace our blood with the blood of an animal, all we could do was pray for mercy.

After the Temple was destroyed, Hadrian began building a new city in Jerusalem, called it Aelia Capitolina, and put a pagan temple in it. This greatly angered the conquered Jewish population. When Hadrian went to Greece in the summer of 132 C.E., the Jews used the opportunity to revolt against the Romans. The war lasted three-and-a-half years. Julius Severus was the general who fought the campaign against the Jews. Instead of directly engaging in battle, he preferred to blockade the Jewish fighters in their fortresses and starve them before defeating them. He was finally successful, and the losses to the Jewish population were enormous. It is against this background of the spiritual, economic, and human devastation of the Temple's destruction and the Bar Kokhba revolt that the dictates of Usha must be seen.

After Hadrian's death, many laws against the Jews were eased and the sages could begin to rebuild the Jewish people spiritually. To that end, they convened a conference in Usha (near Haifa in modern-day Israel) and issued several *takkanot*, or rulings. Many of these, as can be seen in this passage, involve the strengthening of the family. When economic and political times are tough, people may be tempted to separate from their families because they cannot provide for them properly. The sages, by means of these *takkanot*, were clearly attempting to prevent such a thing from happening. So they ordained that a man must support his young children. Some of the methods recorded in this passage for shaming a man who does not support his children are quite inventive and might be taken to heart by today's family courts. As we see, there was no law absolutely mandating this sort of support for children, but the sages enforced it as the right thing to do nonetheless. We also have here rulings about how to educate children.

This passage is a source for the famous principle that one should not give so much to charity that one comes to need charity oneself (p. 118, line 6–p. 119, line 1). The passage ends by relating the rulings of Usha to verses from Psalms in a beautiful way (p. 124, line 4–

p. 125, line 7). Note how the continuation of the generations, and the Torah in those generations, is seen as the sign of peace and well-being. Against the background of slaughter and destruction brought on by the Bar Kokhba revolt, it seems as if the Sages are saying, "Enough of soldiers and arms as ways of trying to maintain the Jewish people. Let us concentrate on children and Torah if we really want to survive." As always, in Jewish life there must be a balance: there are times when an army is a necessity in national life and there are times when the focus must be on the personal and spiritual. The trick is balancing these two factors.

What is really interesting is that *takkanot* (see the *Reference Guide*, p. 274, column 2, 3rd and 4th entries) are just decrees of the sages. They are not derived from Biblical laws but are laid down as necessary rulings in response to the times. (A similar sort of enactment in Germany and France in the tenth century was made, prohibiting polygamy even though it was still "legal" under Jewish law and, indeed, was practiced in far-flung Jewish communities into this century.) In other words, sometimes we must legislate in our own generation what will be good for the Jewish people. Jewish legal creativity is nothing new and is sometimes necessary to preserve the Jewish people.[35]

24. A WIFE'S OBLIGATIONS TO HER HUSBAND

Ketubot 59b–60a
Volume X, page 273, line 4–page 280, line 15
Difficulty Factor: 2

What is the Jewish conception of marriage? More specifically, what is the Jewish ideal of the role "wife"? The answers to these questions presented in this passage may help us understand how we answer these questions today. This is one of those passages that, if you allow it, will serve as a good opening for discussion. If you

---

35. To understand the times that the sages were dealing with after the destruction of the Temple and the Bar Kokhba revolt, imagine what rulings you would have to set down for Judaism and your Jewish community to survive after (God forbid!) a nuclear attack.

don't allow it (i.e., if you can't get past being mad at the sages for some of the sexist things they say), then it won't be such a pleasant or productive experience. You don't have to deny the sexism or suppress your anger at it, but you can't let it blind you to the value of the material.

This is a great passage to study if you want to contrast the theoretical worldview of the Mishnah and the far more realistic worldview of the Gemara. The Mishnah that begins this passage outlines the duties a wife is obligated to perform for her husband.[36] It all sounds so neat and orderly. But the Gemara promptly shows us how complicated the marital relationship actually was. Think of it this way: the Mishnah is like a dream and the Gemara is like psychotherapy, probing the dream, analyzing it, and bringing it into the daylight life of a person.

This passage contains a detailed discussion of nursing (p. 276, line 7–p. 280, line 15): who should nurse, for how long, and the development of a baby's attachment to its mother. In the ancient world, upper-class women would give their babies over to wet nurses rather than nurse the children themselves. So it seems natural that the House of Shammai would allow a woman to follow her family's custom in this matter, since this school generally represented the upper classes, while the House of Hillel allowed her husband to force her to nurse rather than hire a wet nurse. (A poor man, who was used to women nursing their own children, may have balked at paying for a wet nurse.) Naturally, human milk was the only form of nutrition available to newborns in this era (there were no baby formulas at that time!).

It is interesting that the sages legislate this matter as part of the marital relationship. No doubt there was quite a bit of "Oral Torah" related to nursing and weaning in those days, just as there is today. Sadly, this was not included in the Talmud. This gives us a glimpse of women's history that we have lost through time because it was not recorded and preserved. Doubtless, a "women's Gemara" would contain stories of pregnancy, childbirth, nursing,

---

36. The corresponding Mishnah with a husband's duties is on 46b (p. 74, line 4–p. 75, line 1 in this volume) of this tractate.

and motherhood, just as the Gemara we have preserves legends of the sages pursuing their own interests.[37]

25. HOW OFTEN TO HAVE SEX AND LOVE STORIES OF THE SAGES

Ketubot 61b
Volume X, page 306, line 6–page 328, line 8
Difficulty Factor: 3

Even though this passage has been marked as one of medium difficulty, some of it, notably the love stories of the sages, is as easy as Talmudic material can be and is quite inspirational. Therefore, you might want to skim through this passage until you reach the easily understood stories if you are just starting, for these tales are quite lovely.[38]

To understand our passage, we must remember that a husband is obligated to provide his wife with sexual intercourse as part of their marriage agreement, along with her food and clothing. This is not only for the sake of procreation but for his wife's pleasure. The Mishnah (p. 306, line 6–p. 308, line 4), with its propensity to quantify mitzvot, wants to know exactly how often the husband is to provide this service, or at least offer it, to his wife and if there are any conditions that mitigate against living up to this obligation. Does it seem reasonable that everything was as neat and regulated in real life as this Mishnah makes it appear? Real life may have corresponded to this ideal occasionally, but one doubts that intimate relations were so mechanized.

In this Mishnah and its Gemara, we get a nice glimpse of the different classes of men. Obviously, one could not have sex often if one was not in the same town as one's wife or if one worked at a

---

37. See Susan Starr Sered's *Women as Ritual Experts* for more insight into this issue of women's religious traditions (see the For Further Reading section).

38. In addition, if you are interested in modern scholarship on the Talmud, you might want to read about this passage in Daniel Boyarin's book *Carnal Israel: Reading Sex in Talmudic Culture* (see the For Further Reading section), pp. 134–166.

job that demanded so much physical energy that there was none left at the end of the day. These considerations explain why certain groups of men were obligated to have sex less frequently than others.

We note that, like members of Congress exempting themselves from the very laws they make, scholars are given certain dispensations with regard to this Mishnah's rulings (p. 307, line 3). As Boyarin brings out, for the sages, Torah is "the other woman." Were the sages occasionally "workaholics" in their pursuit of Torah, neglecting their family lives to pursue their "careers"? That is one way to read this passage. However, Torah study is not just a career, as you have no doubt found through your own study of Talmud. It is so enriching that the Talmud becomes like a life partner. What is heartening is that the sages did not ever recommend a life of celibacy for scholars. The ideal sage was to have a spouse and children as well as a full-bodied love of Talmud. A love of Talmud is to be balanced with a love of family.

The story of Rabbi Akiva and his wife Rachel (p. 325, line 8–p. 327, line 10) is extremely romantic. It is also inspiring because it shows how, from an illiterate shepherd, a great sage developed. When you are feeling discouraged about your Talmud studies, read this passage and take heart! If Rabbi Akiva started with so little background and achieved so much, you can, too.

Perhaps it was Rachel who inspired Abigail Adams to write, on December 23, 1782, regarding her husband's years of diplomatic work in France and England (1779–1784):

"If you had known," said a person to me the other day, "that Mr. Adams would have remained so long abroad, would you have consented that he should have gone?" I recollected myself a moment and then spoke the real dictates of my heart: "If I had known, sir, that Mr. Adams could have effected what he has done, I would not only have submitted to the absence I have endured, painful as it has been, but I would not have opposed it, even though three years more should be added to the number (which Heaven avert!). I feel a pleasure in being able to sacrifice my selfish passions to the general good, and in imitating the example which has taught me to consider myself and family but as the small dust of the balance, when compared with the great community." (Quoted in Daniel J. Boorstin's *Hidden History: Exploring Our Secret Past* [New York: Vintage Books, 1987], p. 37)

4

Materials from Volumes Still to Come

At the time this guide is being written, only five chapters of *Ketubot* have been translated by Rabbi Steinsaltz. In forthcoming volumes from this tractate some very appealing material will be presented. Since the exact page and line numbers are not available at this time, the passages are cited according to their locations on the traditional page of the Babylonian Talmud folia. General descriptions of these passages are given, as well as some background material. Obviously, there is less detail than in the foregoing passages, since Rabbi Steinsaltz's actual translation and commentary are not before me at this time.

26. HOW TO GIVE CHARITY

Ketubot, chapter 6, from the Mishnah near the bottom
of 67a and the Gemara to it, until the next Mishnah
in the middle of 68a
Difficulty Factor: 2

> *This passage is rated as one of medium difficulty, but most of it is quite easy. It is largely composed of stories about the sages and the way they gave charity.*

When you first read this passage, the sages' tendency to indulge the needy may seem strange. And yet, their ruling is sound. Charity is not just given to sustain the body but to sustain a person's character and individualism as well. A person who receives charity is still a person and still has honor and a distinct personality. In all their giving of charity, these stories tell us, the sages were careful to preserve the dignity of indigent persons.

One interesting part of this passage is the story of Mar Ukba and his wife. It brings up a very important principle in the Talmud: virtue is power. If a woman has more virtue than a man, as in this story, then she is more powerful than a man.

27. HOW TO DEAL WITH PERSONS WITH A DREAD DISEASE

Ketubot, chapter 7, 77b near the top of the page
to the end of 77b
Difficulty Factor: 2

> *Some issues are eternal. For example, how to deal with the fear of death and the role Torah can play in that process were important to the sages and are still important to us today. This passage shows how the sages coped with these dilemmas.*

For the sages, disease and sickness were terrible and potent forces, and the sages were almost powerless to check the processes of illness when compared with physicians today. Today we can separate ourselves from someone who has a contagious disease, by using masks, gloves, and the like. In ancient days, however, being near a person with an infectious disease took great courage. This passage, about the dread, contagious disease *ra'atan* and the compassion one sage showed to its sufferers, could speak very well to our generation and our attitude toward persons with AIDS, for example.

Rabbi Yehoshua ben Levi would sit and study Torah near such sufferers, trusting in the merit of Torah study to protect him. For his great compassion to the sufferers of *ra'atan*, Rabbi Yehoshua ben Levi was allowed to see his place in the World to Come. Indeed, in the process, he was almost able to completely vanquish the Angel of Death. However, a voice from heaven comes forth and decrees that the Angel of Death must be allowed to do his work. Rabbi Ḥanina b. Pappa, who did not study Torah in the company of *ra'atan* sufferers, has great merit, but not so great as that of Rabbi Yehoshua ben Levi. You might want to compare this story of a pillar of fire with that in passage #2.

The concept of the *bat kol*, the heavenly voice, is an important one. It can refer to any of the following four concepts: (1) popular opinion; (2) listening to children, especially asking them what verse they are reading and taking it as prophecy; (3) an echo: *bat kol* can be taken literally as "the daughter of a sound"; (4) *bat kol min hashamayim*: a voice from heaven. This, however, cannot be used as a basis for adjudicating Jewish law. Today the concept of the *bat kol* may be difficult for us to understand since we see our president on television every day and hear his voice all the time. In ancient days, the king lived within the palace and the average person would rarely have heard the king's voice itself and would know the king's will through announcements made by court functionaries. Since the sages believed that earthly courts were a diminished mirror of the heavenly court above, the *bat kol* was the corollary of these announcements made on behalf of the king.

What can we learn from this passage today? First of all, the healing of dread diseases was a matter of religious importance. Traditions about cures were passed on as important religious information. More than that, while the law does not require that we stay with those who have deadly, contagious diseases, and we have many examples of sages who avoided such persons, this story conveys to us how great is our eternal reward if we overcome our fear and are filled with compassion for such persons.

28. DYING WITH DIGNITY

Ketubot, chapter 12, 103a about two-thirds down the page until the next Mishnah on 104a
Difficulty Factor: 2

> *This is one of the most beautiful passages in all of Rabbinic literature. It is tremendously comforting in its portrayal of love, suffer-*

*ing, and death. It would be a good choice for those who are dealing
with terminal illness for it shows how one great sage, and those
around him, coped with his painful death.*

This is the story of Rabbi Yehudah HaNasi's death. He was the
chief authority of his generation. Although personally wealthy,
he lived simply and sustained many students by his charity. He
completed the compilation of the Mishnah begun by Rabbi Akiva.
Rabbi, as he is known, was one of the greatest leaders the Jewish
people ever knew, and it is natural that many legends were told
about his death. These legends can teach us much about how to
stand suffering and how to die with dignity.

The passage begins with a Baraita that details Rabbi's will about
how his closest relationships should be carried on after his death.
There is then a detailed, line-by-line analysis of this Baraita. Then
there is another short passage, wherein Rabbi hands over the reins
of power in the Academy and, again, there is a line-by-line analysis
of it. As part of this analysis, we learn that a man who regularly
visited Rabbi, but who did not do so on the day Rabbi died, apparently committed suicide and was not condemned for it in the heavenly realm. This is just one instance in this whole long passage in
which the usually quite-high value on life in Judaism is balanced
with a need to either achieve merit in the World to Come or end
suffering in this world. As we have mentioned before, values in
Rabbinic literature are balanced one against another, and this passage seems to emphasize the value of death as a way to end spiritual or physical suffering. Obviously, Rabbi's death was a great
historical moment. Are there turning points in history that change
the participants as a group? What would be an analogous event in
our time? President Kennedy's death? Chernobyl?

Next, the second of Rabbi's decrees, about the roles different
persons would play in the Academy, is explored. Obviously, there
was some controversy and competition about these appointments.
Parenthetically, we note that a physical disability did not bar Levi
from being an eminent sage, just as blindness did not prevent
other sages (e.g., Rav Sheshet and Rav Yosef) from attaining greatness. There seems to be a particularly strong controversy about
Rabbi Ḥiyya's not being appointed since he was generally recognized to be a pious, wise sage.

What is really interesting about this passage, though, is that it gives you a chance to see how parallel texts occur in the Bavli. Compare the passage about Rabbi Ḥiyya's argument with Rabbi Ḥanina here and in #18 (*Bava Metzia* 85b; Steinsaltz Edition, volume V, p. 142, line 6–p. 143, line 11). They are identical. In each case, the story is brought to underscore two things: Rabbi Ḥiyya's righteousness and the effectiveness of his method in preserving the Torah, that is, teaching children Torah and Mishnah rather than concentrating on reasoning. The passages are brought in each location as well-known examples of Rabbi Ḥiyya's piety and practice and are inserted as set pieces into the texts. There is nothing terribly fascinating about the use of this passage in two places here. Both uses are germane and easily understandable. It is when the transmission of the passage from place to place involves changes in the text in order to shape it to fit its context that these comparisons can be quite valuable. Indeed, the apparent confusion about who died first, Rabbi or Rabbi Ḥiyya, is augmented by the material from passage #18 (*Bava Metzia* 85b). It is possible to read the material there to imply that Rabbi Ḥiyya had already died while Rabbi was still living.[1] There is probably no way to know exactly what happened, and we should be very cautious about drawing conclusions from the stories preserved for us in the Gemara. What we can glean from our sources is that Rabbi Ḥiyya was one of Rabbi's greatest students. The actual reasons why he was not chosen by Rabbi for leadership are probably lost to us, though the echoes of the controversy engendered by that decision remain.

On the top of 104a we find the extremely famous passage about Rabbi's maid. She is one of the best-known women in Rabbinic literature. Though apparently not formally educated, her opinions, directives, and prayers carried great weight. This story brings up many questions that are important today. Can we pray for people to die when they are suffering? Can we stop taking those measures that are prolonging their lives and their pain? Was Rabbi's maid justified in stopping the sages' prayers in order that Rabbi might die?

---

1. Try taking out both volumes and compare these passages. What is the truth? Who do you think died first, Rabbi or Rabbi Ḥiyya?

Finally, we have the teaching of Rabbi Elazar about angels accompanying the dead. When a person dies there is a sensation of great change. Have you felt this phenomenon of angels, of a presence, when someone dies? This passage would be useful in helping a person who is attracted to the current talk of angels in popular culture and labors under the delusion that Judaism does not believe in angels. Judaism includes within it almost every form of religious expression, be it rationalistic, mystical, social-action-oriented, or as an aid in personal development. There is no reason for Jews to search for these paths to spiritual growth in other faiths.[2]

29. ON THE DANGERS OF TAKING BRIBES

Ketubot, chapter 13, 105a middle of the page–105b
near the bottom
Difficulty Factor: 3

Would you rather be respected or loved? How far must we go to avoid the appearance of, and the actual fact of, a conflict of interest? These are the questions addressed by the stories in this passage. They show how far the sages would go in their pursuit of fairness.

We begin with the story of a judge named Karna who used to charge litigants a fee before pronouncing his verdict. The ensuing argument about his behavior gives us insight into the lives of the sages. They were not professional judges but had to take time off from their "real" jobs in order to listen to these cases. It would seem just that they be compensated for their lost work time. However, such fees might give the appearance of impropriety, and this greatly concerned the sages, for bribe taking is condemned in

---

2. This passage is an ideal one to use in order to examine the way commentary to a basic story has been interpolated into the text itself. Read through the material a few times, perhaps using highlighting pens, and delineate for yourself the stories and the commentaries to them. This may make the passage easier to understand. You might then want to read all the "base" materials, that is, the stories upon which the commentaries are laid, by themselves, and then again with the commentaries to try to get a feel for the way the Talmud developed.

Jewish sources from the Torah on down. There follows an extended Midrashic passage about the dangers of taking bribes, along with many stories on the same subject. (Rabbis, take note of Abaye's words on 105b: a Jewish leader should not strive to be loved at the expense of telling people what they need to hear.)

30. ON THE MERITS OF THE LAND OF ISRAEL AND THE WORLD TO COME

Ketubot, chapter 13, 110b near the bottom–112b
the end of the tractate
Difficulty Factor: 4

> *This is a very long passage, most of which is quite easy. It would be a great thing to study before (or after) one went on a trip to Israel or for a Zionist-oriented group's study program (e.g., ZOA, Hadassah, Federation, etc.). It is all about the merits of the Land of Israel and its place in Jewish thought and religion. It is rated a "4" because some of the Midrashim are pretty fanciful and, as of this writing, without Rabbi Steinsaltz's commentary, they are a bit difficult to understand.*

We begin with the Baraita about the desirability of living in the Land of Israel. Obviously, sages who lived in Babylonia might feel a bit ambivalent about subscribing to the merits of the Land of Israel while choosing to live elsewhere. How did they cope with these feelings? They made Babylonia second only to the Land of Israel (Rav Yehudah's statement in the name of Shmuel). Similarly, today, we might admit that the fullest Jewish life can be lived in Israel but that America is second only to Israel in the quality of its Jewish life and that one should not move from America to, say, the island of Tristan in the South Atlantic if one wants to live in a robust Jewish community.

With Abaye's statement that Babylonia will not witness the turbulent times that will precede the Messiah's coming, the passage now turns toward a consideration of the World to Come and the ultimate redemption of the world. The connection should be obvious: of all places on earth, Israel is deemed closest to heaven, just as, of all times on earth, Shabbat is considered a taste of the World to Come. Thus, the entire tractate moves into a grand summation, called a *neḥemta*, about holiness and redemption in this world and the next.

These images of the World to Come—the underground tunnels whereby the righteous will roll to Israel, the way the dead will rise up from the ground, and the manner in which the Land will produce incredibly abundant food—might sound like fairy tales. We can understand them as representing the dearest hopes of the sages in those days. Today, we do not have to dream of a quick method of directly getting to a place. We have subways and airplanes. We do not have to dream of bountiful crops. We have fertilizers that yield tomatoes of three pounds each. *Our* hopes for the future are reflected in programs like "Star Trek." In our vision of Redemption, we'll all be transported (*à la* "Beam us up, Scottie!") to the Land of Israel and food will be prepared and served by computers. Just imagine how terrific Redemption will *actually* be if this is the best we can imagine it!

The long section that follows details the great fertility of the Land of Israel. Here is a case where the fantasy-like claims of the Talmud are close to becoming a reality. Anyone who has visited a *kibbutz* in the Negev desert and seen the flowers blooming out of that arid wilderness will recognize the sages' dreams come true. The Land—with the help of hard work and modern technology— is fertile beyond belief. Is it any less of a miracle because God and human beings work together to bring it about?

The very last part of this tractate shows so perfectly what the Talmud is all about. On the one hand, it predicts that the process of bringing the Messiah will be filled with trials and tribulations, particularly for the sages themselves. On the other hand, this is followed by a prediction that when the Messiah comes, even wild trees will bear fruit and not, as we would expect, only cultivated trees. So we have a time of turmoil and a time of peace juxtaposed, a time of hardship and a time of plenty. The Talmud refuses to choose because both predictions are part of reality and, therefore, part of redemption. We note, however, that the opinion cited last in a passage is usually the one the sages wish to emphasize. So we end with hope for the plenty and peace of the World to Come.

For Further Reading

A s the Talmud speaks in seventy tongues, you should feel free to attend to that language of the Talmud that speaks to you most clearly. Obviously, this will change as you develop as a Talmud student. It is often productive to alternate between straightforward textual study, as with the Steinsaltz English Talmud, and with secondary literature. This secondary literature is vast and can speed your process of understanding the Talmud by allowing you to become more quickly familiar with the world of the sages. It can also help you understand the Talmud and Rabbinic literature by focusing on these topics through the lenses of other modern disciplines, such as literary criticism or anthropology. Below are some suggestions for further reading.

Aries, Philippe and Georges Duby, editors. *A History of Private Life From Pagan Rome to Byzantium*. Cambridge: Belknap Press, 1987.
A beautiful, illustrated, easy-to-read volume that can provide you with some background about the Roman world in which much of Rabbinic literature was written.

Bialik, Hayim and Yehoshua Ravnitzky, editors. Transl., William Braude. *The Book of Legends*. New York: Schocken, 1992.
This is an absolutely invaluable resource, only recently available in translation. The original work, in Hebrew, took stories from Rabbinic literature and organized them according to subject. Thus, for example, if you wanted to look up the most famous stories about Rabbi Akiva or what Rabbinic literature

143

says about the relationship between husband and wife, all you had to do was look up the topic rather than search through the Talmud. This is a great way to follow up on a subject that stimulates your interest while studying the Talmud or to find out additional background information about one of the sages.

Boyarin, Daniel. *Carnal Israel: Reading Sex in Talmudic Culture.* Berkeley, CA: University of California Press, 1993.
   This is a very scholarly book (read: a bit difficult to understand) about attitudes toward sexuality in the Talmud. It's worth the effort it takes.

Carmell, Aryeh. *Aids to Talmud Study.* New York: Feldheim, 1980.
   A slim, easy-to-use reference volume for the beginner.

Cohen, Stuart A. *The Three Crowns: Structures of Communal Politics in Early Rabbinic Jewry.* New York: Cambridge University Press, 1990.
   If you're into politics and power struggles as the way you understand things, then this is your book on the Talmud. Cohen traces the balance of power in the Jewish world through the Rabbinic era and shows the tension between the Davidic line, the priesthood, and the sages.

Eilberg-Schwartz, Howard. *The Savage in Judaism: An Anthropology of Israelite Religion and Ancient Judaism.* Bloomington, IN: Indiana University Press, 1990.
   This is the book for those who like an anthropological approach. The author explains key concepts in Rabbinic literature, such as the priesthood and ritual impurity, in a way that makes them clear and meaningful.

Encyclopaedia Judaica. Jerusalem: Keter, 1972.
   The standard Jewish reference work. You'll find an article about almost anything in which you're interested. Available in most synagogue and college libraries.

Epstein, I., ed. *The Babylonian Talmud.* London: Soncino Press, 1936.

Goodblatt, David M. *Rabbinic Instruction in Sasanian Babylonia.* Leiden: Brill, 1975.

This is a technical but very interesting exploration of the different systems sages used to convey wisdom in Babylonia and the Land of Israel.

Hammer, Reuven, transl. *Sifre on Deuteronomy.* New Haven, CT: Yale University Press, 1986.

The beautiful, lucid, and well-annotated translation of this early Midrash to the Book of Deuteronomy.

Katz, Jacob. *Exclusiveness and Tolerance: Studies in Jewish–Gentile Relations in Medieval and Modern Times.* New York: Behrman House, 1961.

This slim, readable volume shows how many of the laws in the Talmud developed and changed over the centuries.

Kraemer, David. *The Mind of the Talmud: An Intellectual History of the Bavli.* New York: Oxford University Press, 1990.

If you are into debate and discussion and literary analysis of the Talmud, this is the volume to read. It traces how different layers of the Bavli developed and explains the Bavli's tendency to give us alternatives rather than prescriptions.

Sered, Susan Starr. *Women as Ritual Experts: The Religious Lives of Elderly Jewish Women in Jerusalem.* New York: Oxford University Press, 1992.

This is a wonderful book that chronicles women's religious lives and the way they differ from men's. It gives us a way of searching the Talmud for information about women's spiritual lives 2,000 years ago.

Steinsaltz, Adin. *The Strife of the Spirit.* Northvale, NJ: Jason Aronson, 1988.

In addition to everything else, Rabbi Steinsaltz writes beautiful, imaginative stories related to Rabbinic literature that can help a new student develop a foothold in the foreign land the sages inhabited.

————. *The Talmud: The Steinsaltz Edition.* New York: Random House, 1989.

————. *The Thirteen Petalled Rose.* Northvale, NJ: Jason Aronson, 1992.
This slim volume is Rabbi Steinsaltz's introduction to mysticism. This is very intense reading and though it's only 181 pages long, be prepared to spend several weeks (at least!) making your way through it.

Strack, H. L. and G. Stemberger. *Introduction to the Talmud and Midrash.* Edinburgh: T & T Clark, 1991.
This is the ideal, one-volume reference work for the student of Rabbinic literature. It summarizes current scholarship as it informs you about where, when, and by whom different works of Rabbinic literature were written.

An Invitation

Are you currently studying Talmud?

If so, we'd like to hear from you. Please send us a letter describing your study activity and we'll share it with readers in the next edition of this book. Send your description to:

Maqom: A Place for the Spiritually Searching
P.O. Box 31900–323
Houston, TX 77231

**Would you like help starting a Talmud study group
or finding a teacher?**

If so, contact the Talmud Circle Project for help:

Talmud Circle Project
c/o Aleph Society
25 West 45th Street, Suite #1409
New York, NY 10036–4902

Index

About the Author

Judith Z. Abrams is a woman with a mission: she wants to bring the beauty of Talmud to as many people, and with as much depth, as possible. To that end, she has published four books on the Talmud (*The Talmud for Beginners*, volumes I and II, *The Women of the Talmud*, and with her husband, Dr. Steven A. Abrams, *Jewish Parenting: Rabbinic Insights*), earned her Ph.D. in rabbinic literature from the Baltimore Hebrew University, and teaches across the country. She is the founder and director of *Maqom*: A Place for the Spiritually Searching, a school for adult Talmud study where anyone can learn, regardless of their background. She lives in Houston with her husband, Steven, and their three children, Michael, Ruth, and Hannah.